Critical Reflection
and the
Foreign Language Classroom

Critical Studies in Education and Culture Series

Literacy in the Library: Negotiating the Spaces Between Order and Desire
Mark Dressman

Thinking Again: Education After Postmodernism
Nigel Blake, Paul Smeyers, Richard Smith, and Paul Standish

Racial Categorization of Multiracial Children in Schools
Jane Ayers Chiong

bell hooks' Engaged Pedagogy: Education for Critical Consciousness
Namulundah Florence

Wittgenstein: Philosophy, Postmodernism, Pedagogy
Michael Peters and James Marshall

Policy, Pedagogy, and Social Inequality: Community College Student Realities in Post-Industrial America
Penelope E. Herideen

Psychoanalysis and Pedagogy
Stephen Appel, editor

The Rhetoric of Diversity and the Traditions of American Literary Study: Critical Multiculturalism in English
Lesliee Antonette

Becoming and Unbecoming White: Owning and Disowning a Racial Identity
Christine Clark and James O'Donnell

Critical Pedagogy: An Introduction, 2nd Edition
Barry Kanpol

Michel Foucault: Materialism and Education
Mark Olssen

Revolutionary Social Transformation: Democratic Hopes, Political Possibilities, and Critical Education
Paula Allman

Critical Reflection
and the
Foreign Language Classroom

Terry A. Osborn

Critical Studies in Education and Culture Series
Edited by Henry A. Giroux

INFORMATION AGE
PUBLISHING

Greenwich, Connecticut 06830 • www.infoagepub.com

Library of Congress Cataloging-in-Publication Data

Osborn, Terry A., 1966–
Critical reflection and the foreign language classroom / Terry A.
    Osborn.
        p. cm.—(Critical studies in education and culture series.
    ISSN 1064–8615)
        Includes bibliographical references (p.) and index.
        ISBN 0–89789–681–5 (alk. paper)
        1. Language and languages—Study and teaching—United States.
    I. Title. II. Series.
    P57.U7078 2000
    418'.0071'073—dc21   99–40323

British Library Cataloguing in Publication Data is available.

Library of Congress Catalog Card Number: 99–40323
ISBN: 0–89789–681–5
ISSN: 1064–8615

First published in 2000

Bergin & Garvey, 88 Post Road West, Westport, CT 06881
An imprint of Greenwood Publishing Group, Inc.
www.greenwood.com

Published in paperback by arrangement with Greenwood Publishing Group, Inc.
Westport, CT.

Paperback version copyright © 2005 by IAP—Information Age Publishing, Inc.

ISBN: 1–59311–313–7

Printed in the United States of America

10 9 8 7 6 5 4 3 2 1

Copyright Acknowledgment

Portions of the following text are reprinted with permission:

National Standards in Foreign Language Education Project. 1996. *Standards for foreign language
learning: Preparing for the 21st century.* Lawrence, KS: Allen Press.

For Dina, Joshua, and Juliana

my beloved

Contents

Figures

Acknowledgments

The list of those who have assisted me in producing this text could never be complete. Many language teachers, colleagues, and students I have known have added something very real, if intangible, to this current project. I would like to extend my gratitude specifically to Henry A. Giroux for his support of the text and his recognition of the importance of understanding the politics of schooling in world language education. Steven Kercel and Nancy Lauckner were helpful in contributing ideas for examples in the text. I want to thank Jacqueline Davis and Magnus Bassey for their input and careful reading of chapter drafts. Timothy Reagan, as well, has provided valuable feedback and criticism. My colleagues at Queens College, CUNY, have provided unyielding support in my pursuit of incorporating the ideas in this text into our teacher preparation program, and in providing me the time needed to complete this work. Jane Garry has been helpful and supportive in navigating the particulars of publication. My family has indubitably contributed the most, though, by understanding why I was locked away for so many hours staring at a computer, and willingly making the sacrifice.

Series Foreword

Educational reform has fallen upon hard times. The traditional assumption that schooling is fundamentally tied to the imperatives of citizenship designed to educate students to exercise civic leadership and public service has been eroded. The schools are now the key institution for producing professional, technically trained, credentialized workers for whom the demands of citizenship are subordinated by the vicissitudes of the marketplace and the commercial public sphere. Given the current corporate and right wing assault on public and higher education, coupled with the emergence of a moral and political climate that has shifted to a new Social Darwinism, the issues which framed the democratic meaning, purpose, and use to which education might aspire have been displaced by more vocational and narrowly ideological considerations.

The war waged against the possibilities of an education wedded to the precepts of a real democracy is not merely ideological. Against the backdrop of reduced funding for public schooling, the call for privatization, vouchers, cultural uniformity, and choice, there are the often ignored larger social realities of material power and oppression. On the national level, there has been a vast resurgence of racism. This is evident in the passing of anti-immigration laws such as Proposition 187 in Cali-

fornia, the dismantling of the welfare state, the demonization of black
youth that is taking place in the popular media, and the remarkable attention provided by the media to forms of race talk that argue for the intellectual inferiority of blacks or dismiss calls for racial justice as simply a
holdover from the "morally bankrupt" legacy of the 1960s.

Poverty is on the rise among children in the United States, with 20
percent of all children under the age of eighteen living below the poverty line. Unemployment is growing at an alarming rate for poor youth
of color, especially in the urban centers. While black youth are policed
and disciplined in and out of the nation's schools, conservative and liberal educators define education through the ethically limp discourses of
privatization, national standards, and global competitiveness.

Many writers in the critical education tradition have attempted to
challenge the right wing fundamentalism behind educational and social
reform in both the United States and abroad while simultaneously providing ethical signposts for a public discourse about education and democracy that is both prophetic and transformative. Eschewing traditional categories, a diverse number of critical theorists and educators
have successfully exposed the political and ethical implications of the
cynicism and despair that has become endemic to the discourse of
schooling and civic life. In its place, such educators strive to provide a language of hope that inextricably links the struggle over schooling to understanding and transforming our present social and cultural dangers.

At the risk of overgeneralizing, both cultural studies theorists and
critical educators have emphasized the importance of understanding
theory as the grounded basis for "intervening into contexts and
power . . . in order to enable people to act more strategically in ways that
may change their context for the better."[1] Moreover, theorists in both
fields have argued for the primacy of the political by calling for and
struggling to produce critical public spaces, regardless of how fleeting
they may be, in which "popular cultural resistance is explored as a form
of political resistance."[2] Such writers have analyzed the challenges that
teachers will have to face in redefining a new mission for education, one
that is linked to honoring the experiences, concerns, and diverse histo-
ries and languages that give expression to the multiple narratives that
engage and challenge the legacy of democracy.

Equally significant is the insight of recent critical educational work
that connects the politics of difference with concrete strategies for addressing the crucial relationships between schooling and the economy,

and citizenship and the politics of meaning in communities of multicultural, multiracial, and multilingual schools.

Critical Studies in Education and Culture attempts to address and demonstrate how scholars working in the fields of cultural studies and the critical pedagogy might join together in a radical project and practice informed by theoretically rigorous discourses that affirm the critical but refuse the cynical, and establish hope as central to a critical pedagogical and political practice but eschew a romantic utopianism. Central to such a project is the issue of how pedagogy might provide cultural studies theorists and educators with an opportunity to engage pedagogical practices that are not only transdisciplinary, transgressive, and oppositional, but also connected to a wider project designed to further racial, economic, and political democracy.[3] By taking seriously the relations between culture and power, we further the possibilities of resistance, struggle, and change.

Critical Studies in Education and Culture is committed to publishing work that opens a narrative space that affirms the contextual and the specific while simultaneously recognizing the ways in which such spaces are shot through with issues of power. The series attempts to continue an important legacy of theoretical work in cultural studies in which related debates on pedagogy are understood and addressed within the larger context of social responsibility, civic courage, and the reconstruction of democratic public life. We must keep in mind Raymond Williams's insight that the "deepest impulse (informing cultural politics) is the desire to make learning part of the process of social change itself."[4] Education as a cultural pedagogical practice takes place across multiple sites, which include not only schools and universities but also the mass media, popular culture, and other public spheres, and signals how within diverse contexts, education makes us both subjects of and subject to relations of power.

This series challenges the current return to the primacy of market values and simultaneous retreat from politics so evident in the recent work of educational theorists, legislators, and policy analysts. Professional relegitimation in a troubled time seems to be the order of the day as an increasing number of academics both refuse to recognize public and higher education as critical public spheres and offer little or no resistance to the ongoing vocationalization of schooling, the continuing evisceration of the intellectual labor force, and the current assaults on the working poor, the elderly, and women and children.[5]

Emphasizing the centrality of politics, culture, and power, *Critical Studies in Education and Culture* will deal with pedagogical issues that contribute in imaginative and transformative ways to our understanding of how critical knowledge, democratic values, and social practices can provide a basis for teachers, students, and other cultural workers to redefine their role as engaged and public intellectuals. Each volume will attempt to rethink the relationship between language and experience, pedagogy and human agency, and ethics and social responsibility as part of a larger project for engaging and deepening the prospects of democratic schooling in a multiracial and multicultural society. *Critical Studies in Education and Culture* takes on the responsibility of witnessing and addressing the most pressing problems of public schooling and civic life, and engages culture as a crucial site and strategic force for productive social change.

Henry A. Giroux

NOTES

1. Lawrence Grossberg, "Toward a Genealogy of the State of Cultural Studies," in Cary Nelson and Dilip Parameshwar Gaonkar, eds. *Disciplinarity and Dissent in Cultural Studies* (New York: Routledge, 1996), 143.

2. David Bailey and Stuart Hall, "The Vertigo of Displacement," *Ten 8* 2:3 (1992), 19.

3. My notion of transdisciplinary comes from Mas'ud Zavarzadeh and Donald Morton, "Theory, Pedagogy, Politics: The Crisis of the 'Subject' in the Humanities," in *Theory Pedagogy Politics: Texts for Change*, Mas'ud Zavarzadeh and Donald Morton, eds. (Urbana: University of Illinois Press, 1992), 10. At issue here is neither ignoring the boundaries of discipline-based knowledge nor simply fusing different disciplines, but creating theoretical paradigms, questions, and knowledge that cannot be taken up within the policed boundaries of the existing disciplines.

4. Raymond Williams, "Adult Education and Social Change," in *What I Came to Say* (London: Hutchinson-Radus, 1989), 158.

5. The term "professional legitimation" comes from a personal correspondence with Professor Jeff Williams of East Carolina University.

Foreword

The dawn of the 21st century has witnessed a renewed interest in foreign language teaching in the United States. Many critical teachers committed to social justice would like to see this interest arising from an aspiration to promote understandings of diverse peoples and cultures in the world and to create an equal ground for mutual communication across cultural and linguistic differences. For those teachers, such understandings would hold promise for constructing more just and equal human relations without prejudice, domination, or exploitation. However, the current discourse on the promotion of foreign language study is preoccupied by an emphasis on its benefit for maintaining economic competitiveness in the world and strengthening national security. The notion of economic competitiveness connotes a quest for creating and maintaining an economic hierarchy of power among the rich and the poor. Similarly, the concept of strengthening national security in the U.S. context assumes the nation's self-interest in protecting its hegemony by prevailing over other countries rather than coexisting with them peacefully. Evidently, both are rooted in a metaphor of winning a conflict at the expense of others.

The recent emphasis on economic competitiveness and national security was evident at a June 2004 national language conference sponsored by the Department of Defense and held at the Center for Advanced Study of Language at University of Maryland. Some of the conference documents available on the web (http://www.nlconference.org/) mention the need to provide more instruction in less commonly taught languages such as Arabic, Korean, Pashto, Persian, and Urdu for national strategic reasons. This prompts questions such as: Which languages are regarded as the most important or useful to learn and why? and What political interest triggers the promotion of foreign language teaching? Under the current situation, the answers to these questions are obviously related to the rhetoric of the war on terrorism which was triggered by the events of 9/11 and the following U.S. invasion of Afghanistan and Iraq. This example shows that foreign language teaching is closely related to national and international politics—it is never politically or ideologically neutral. Although some may argue that what is political is only the teaching of the strategically important languages mentioned above, teaching any language is part of the larger foreign language educational agenda which encompasses political, economic, and ideological interests. Whether they like it or not, teachers are always surrounded by politics and ideologies that influence the rationale, content, and emphasis of curriculum and instruction.

While national security and economic competitiveness sound like monstrous notions for teachers to wrestle with, politics and ideologies manifest themselves in more subtle ways in everyday instruction. By presenting certain information about the target culture in an innocuous way, teachers might be perpetuating exotic and essentialized cultural images that do not reflect lived experiences of the diverse people in multiple communities in which the target language is spoken. As Terry Osborn cogently critiques in this book, such cultural exoticism and essentialism would construct and legitimate static images of the *foreigner* as the *Other*, relegating foreign language education in the U.S. to learning only about what is "foreign" juxtaposed with what is "American," which is itself essentialized as White English-speaking culture. This binary neglects the rich linguistic and cultural diversity that U.S. society embraces. The lack of focus on diversity creates a serious contradiction for foreign language education; that is, while foreign language education appears to promote multiculturalism and multilingualism, it actually denies them and instead constructs an essentialist understanding about the culture and language of Self and Other. To this effect, foreign language education directly and indirectly supports the unitary norm of language and culture, seen in the discourses of English only for immigrants and the teaching of the standard prestigious version of the target language, both at home and in the community in which the target language is used.

While such political and ideological aspects of foreign language education need to be scrutinized in order to create alternative educational visions, there have been very few voices that actually challenge them. This is perhaps due to the tendency that, unlike other core subjects or English as a Second Language taught in schools, foreign language courses typically enroll college-bound elite students and thus teachers feel they are immune to sociopolitical or socioeconomic issues that negatively affect the educational success of mainly marginalized students of color and low socioeconomic status. However, a critical understanding of the politics and ideologies of foreign language teaching is essential for professionals for the following compelling reasons. First, college-bound students are likely to take leadership positions in their future careers, influencing cross-cultural understanding and communication in various professional fields. Second, in advocating foreign language education for all students, which many foreign language professionals have been doing, teachers must intellectually engage in complex issues of diversity by asking questions such as: What do we do to support students of color and heritage language learners to achieve equal learning outcomes? What should be the rationale for teaching foreign language to all students? Should it primarily be for immediate job and economic benefits for individuals? Or should it be for fostering critical understandings of various kinds of difference in order to create a more just society in which students socially and politically participate?

These issues and questions address a pursuit of equality and social justice to transform unequal relations of power in terms of race, gender, class, and other social categories. This is what critical pedagogies aim for. Critical pedagogies encourage teachers and students to question all taken-for-granted notions in order to critically reflect on how unequal relations of power seen in the systems of domination and subordination are created and sustained. For instance, teachers can pose such questions as: What linguistic and cultural norms exist in foreign language teaching and learning? How have these norms come to exist? Why are the norms created and legitimated? What are the consequences? Who benefits from creating and perpetuating the norm? Who is oppressed by it? What role do we play as foreign language teachers/learners in supporting or transforming the norm through teaching/learning it?

One of the important aspects of critical pedagogies is the critical understanding of cultural difference. Many foreign language classrooms often address cultural difference by celebrating holidays, customs, and festivals observed in the mainstream target community. However, critical pedagogies do not merely validate cultural traditions but also go beyond the celebration of difference—they address the politics behind cultural traditions and, furthermore, question how cultural difference has been constructed and sustained. Critical teachers would ask such questions as: What diversity exists in celebrating traditions? How have the traditions changed in history? What political interests do the traditions serve? How does the cultural uniqueness seen in traditions get constructed as cultural difference? Who benefits? In exploring these questions, the target cultural is seen not as static, homogeneous, or essentialized but as diverse, dynamic, and always implicated in politics. Critical pedagogies seriously challenge the essentialism and exotic foreignness often constructed in foreign language teaching.

Critical pedagogies have been promoted by a number of scholars in the field of education. Paulo Freire is perhaps the best-known educator and an advocate of critical literacy. Others include scholars such as Henry Giroux, Jennifer Gore, Barry Kanpol, Donaldo Macedo, Peter McLaren, Ira Shor, and Christine Sleeter. In the field of teaching English as a second language and bilingual education, critical pedagogies have been promoted by Elsa Auerbach, Sarah Benesch, Suresh Canagarajah, Jim Cummins, Angel Lin, Brian Morgan, and Alastair Pennycook, to name just a few. While these educators and teachers have engaged in active inquiry into critical approaches to teaching and learning for social justice, foreign language teaching by and large has been immune to these approaches. It is extremely rare to hear presentations on critical pedagogies at professional conferences or to see the topic published in books or journals. As a scholar and teacher educator in both foreign language and English as a second language, I was quite frustrated and discouraged by the lack of discussion until this book came out.

Terry Osborn is indeed one of the first scholars and teacher educators to write about important issues in foreign language education from a perspective of critical pedagogies. He critically reflects on the perpetual obsession with *foreignness* in foreign language education which undermines the acknowledgement of multiculturalism and multilingualism that exist within the U.S. This critique should be contemplated seriously, because foreign language professionals are often regarded as supporters of diversity, yet their obsession with *foreignness* normalizes the dominant and essentialized form of culture and language, preventing them from seeing and supporting true diversity at home and abroad. This contradiction needs to be scrutinized by teachers and teacher educators, particularly in the current situation where our society is facing increased demographic diversity at home and a dire need to understand different perspectives abroad. As I mentioned in the beginning, the events of 9/11 have stirred up the discussion on the needs for teaching foreign languages. However, does teaching a language for national security and economic competitiveness prepare citizens to coexist with diverse populations? Will this book's plea for positive social change be accomplished through such rationales? What alternative rationales for teaching languages can be developed based on situated ethics? Foreign language professionals are now positioned in a precarious ideological location, which requires them to engage in active discussions on what missions should be established and what contributions the field can make to the national and international community. This book perfectly serves as a springboard for such important discussions.

—Ryuko Kubota
August, 2004

Chapter 1

Beyond Methodology

The verb *delimit* means "to fix or mark the limits or boundaries of; de-marcate."[1] In the context of language education in the United States, those of us who teach languages other than English have traditionally described our subject as "foreign" languages. This term has become increasingly uncomfortable for language educators, however, as linguistic diversity has grown in the United States. How to delimit what is foreign about languages in the context of the United States is, to say the least, problematic. As a result, the authors of recent curriculum guidelines, standards, and textbooks have searched for alternate adjectives to describe what kind of languages are being taught. Thus, "second languages," "modern languages," "world languages," and sometimes simply "languages" become the appropriate course descriptors.

It is not the term itself that should be of primary concern; rather the focus should be on the concepts and biases that underlie it. Unfortunately, however, language educators in the United States, especially those who have been traditionally referred to as "foreign" language teachers, have most often been ill-prepared to examine the sociological nature of their craft. Teachers of language learn much about applied linguistic theory in terms of language acquisition (Ellis 1990), and much about pedagogy in terms of methodology, but they are rarely called upon to explain the role of the language teacher in a societal context. This text, written by a language educator for language educators, seeks to be a genesis toward rectifying this oversight.

Language teachers in contemporary society need to become critically reflective practitioners. As I am using the term, a critically reflective language teacher is one who is aware, at multiple levels, of the power relationships that exist and shape the content and context of a language course. To become a critically reflective practitioner, however, you the reader will begin by utilizing what seems like yet another "foreign" language. Terms such as *ideology, hegemony,* and *marginalization* will become part of your vocabulary as you develop the eyes and ears of a teacher concerned about social inequality and the role of language education in perpetuating and in challenging such inequality. This text will serve as both a book about critical reflection and a collection of critical reflections on the foreign language classroom.

Awareness alone, however, is insufficient to effect change in the language classrooms of the United States. Teachers need, as well, to explore how to apply this critical understanding in meaningful ways in their classrooms as they continue to meet the curricular imperatives of their courses. In this way, the language classes of the future can be transformed into learning environments in which students begin, to paraphrase Paulo Freire, to read the *palabra* and the *mundo,* the *Wort* and the *Welt,* the *mot* and the *monde,* the *parola* and the *mondo,* the *word* and the *world.*

In this text you will practice skills in critical reflection by examining the concept of *foreignness* in foreign language curricula and textbooks, specifically in terms of how it may play an important role in the production and reproduction of social inequality in the United States. This concept finds its way, ultimately, into the classrooms, curriculum guides, and textbooks that serve a unique gatekeeping function for the educated people in our society. As a result, the concept of *foreignness* can legitimately be considered to be foundational for foreign language teaching in the United States in that it guides presumptions, goals, and outcomes. And unfortunately, by determining how scores of college-educated Americans will delimit *foreignness,* this educational context aids in the continuation of a language environment that clearly favors one group of U.S.-Americans over others.

For teachers of language to first identify, then address, the issue of *foreignness*, however, will require looking both within and beyond the classroom. Teachers of language will need to have a heightened awareness of how issues related to language and power influence, and are influenced by, discourse within a societal context. In other words, it is no longer sufficient to treat the "subject" of language as neutral, apolitical knowledge. Granted, finding political bias in a conjugation or declension seems absurd at first. But I encourage the reader to suspend judgment on that assumption for now. At a minimum, since most courses in language have moved beyond only grammatical instruction, it is easy to see that there are elements other than simple (or complex) grammar that make their way into the language classroom. The purpose of this text is to assist the U.S. language educator in examining all of these elements in terms of the power structures outside the classroom that underlie and support them.

HISTORICAL OVERVIEW

In the context of U.S. secondary education, a standard or prescribed set of courses for students may be most readily traced back to the development of the academy. Replacing the Latin grammar school, the academy, though intended to provide a practical course of study, instead established course guidelines based on a classical curriculum preparing students for college admission (see Brown 1926; Monroe 1940; Ornstein and Hunkins 1993). Of the top fifteen subjects offered in 1828 at the academies, for example, three were foreign languages, growing to four between 1850 and 1875 (Ornstein and Hunkins 1993). The addition was German, due no doubt at least in part to the increase in the German-speaking population from the arrival of the "forty-niners."

Between 1893 and 1895, the National Education Association's (NEA) "Committee of Ten" identified Latin, Greek, and other, modern, languages as central to the standard high school curriculum. In 1918, the NEA Commission on the Reorganization of Secondary Education published the influential *Cardinal Principles of Secondary Education*, further fine-tuning the curriculum to five essential subjects, including modern language. It can be argued that even since the inception of educational institutions in the United States, "foreign" language education has had an important, even central, role to play.

It would be misleading, however, to assume that this central role has been without controversy within society. German-speaking citizens in

1840 in Ohio, for example, lobbied for and won the passage of a law requiring the teaching of German if the number of requests reached seventy-five in one school system. At least seven other states followed the example. In St. Louis, as well, persuaded by a tacit threat of boycott, the board of education initiated German language classes at the elementary level. Enrollment included not only students of German descent, but also Anglo-American pupils. Tyack (1974) refers to this process as "immigrant groups seeking symbolic affirmation of their worth" (108).

The search for symbolic affirmation, however, at times included efforts to exclude other languages. Tyack (1974) reports of a German-American leader who decried the potential inclusion of the languages of Hungarian, Polish, and Italian peoples, while other language groups were successful in introducing curricula into the common school, including Polish, Italian, Czech, Norwegian, French, Spanish, and Dutch. Beginning in the mid-nineteenth century, Dicker (1996) reports, the English-speaking population became increasingly concerned with the explosion of linguistic diversity within the population of the United States. The Edward's law in Illinois (1889) and the Bennett Bill in Wisconsin (1889) attempted to prohibit instruction in languages other than English in both public and private schools. One state made teaching German illegal, another made even speaking German in public a punishable offense (Dicker 1996). Between 1914 and 1917, as the United States was drawn into the conflict of World War I, and thus German became the "enemy's language," the anti-German sentiment escalated to the level of hysteria. Wiley (1998) catalogs the "cultural wars" that ensued: beatings of German speakers, university-sponsored book-burnings, censorship, and religious persecution. Language, and specifically language instructional programs, became central points of focus in regard to the cultural conflict. In 1923, the Supreme Court finally overturned the laws that made teaching non-English languages illegal. Today, less than a century later, despite a growing presence of linguistic minorities in the country, English enjoys a status of de facto, though not de jure, official language of the country, while German classes are becoming increasingly difficult to find.[2]

Though the English language is a national language in the sense that it is most widely used for commerce and governmental functions, its lack of status as an official language, that is, the language legislatively deemed to be used in governmental functions, is germane to education

in a democracy. Public education in a democracy can and should prepare students to function in a national language. At the same time,
however, there is a need to avoid the support of structural monolingualism,[3] which would be inherently discriminatory.

The social context of U.S. language education, then, currently and
historically has demonstrated elements of struggle that are not readily
apparent within the classroom. Part of the elusive nature of the conflicts
surrounding and underlying language education in the United States is
related to the value ascribed education in "foreign" languages. In short,
foreign language education is traditionally held to be valuable due to an
ability to broaden a student's background and cultural perspective.

The British educational philosopher R. S. Peters has argued in a
number of works that the term *education* has three distinct uses: sociological, institutional, and the "general enlightenment" sense. In this
third sense, Hamm (1989) explains, education "is considered to be a
most valuable development of mind characterized by knowledge and
understanding. Such a nascent concept of education was already extant
in early Greece and was referred to as *paedia*" (31). Peters (1975) further notes that associated with the sense of education as general enlightenment are the breadth and depth criteria of knowledge:

> Thus our concept of an educated person is of someone who is ca-
> pable of delighting in a variety of pursuits and projects for their
> own sake and whose pursuit of them and general conduct of his
> life are transformed by some degree of all-round understanding
> and sensitivity. Pursuing the practical is not necessarily a disqualifi-
> cation for being educated; for the practical need not be pursued
> under a purely instrumental aspect. This does not mean, of
> course, that an educated man is oblivious to the instrumental
> value of pursuits—e.g. of science. It means only that he does not
> view them purely under this aspect. Neither does it mean that he
> has no specialized knowledge; it means only that he is not just a
> narrow-minded specialist. (9–10)

Foreign language education, it is often held, helps students become
"well-rounded," and thus it is often presented as an indispensable part
of a liberal arts education.

More recently, however, educators have begun to understand that
knowledge, or what constitutes knowledge, is not simply neutral material. The interests and powers that underlie the production of knowl-

edge in educational contexts have been the subject of increased examination and hypothesizing by curriculum theorists and educators. As Peter McLaren (1989) has asserted, critical pedagogues challenge the notion that schools are places where knowledge alone is passed on:

> Recent advances in the sociology of knowledge, cultural and symbolic anthropology, cultural Marxism, and semiotics have led these theorists to see schools not only as instructional sites, but also as cultural arenas where a heterogeneity of ideological and social forms often collide in an unremitting struggle for dominance. Within this context, critical theorists generally analyze schools in a twofold way: as sorting mechanisms in which select groups of students are favored on the basis of race, class, and gender; and as agencies for self and social empowerment. (160)

Since schools act as sites for sorting and empowering students based on some set of criteria, understanding and even challenging those criteria becomes vitally important for those teachers who are committed to teaching in a democratic society (see Arnowitz and Giroux 1985, 1991).

CONTEMPORARY LANGUAGE EDUCATION AND THE U.S. CONTEXT

Sociologists of language and language educators have commonly contrasted foreign language education with second language education in more general terms (Corson 1990). Eastman (1983) specifically notes that a second language "is one already in the learner's world, whereas a foreign language represents a foreign culture" (93). This definition simply does not apply in the context of the United States, however. It is difficult to understand how one could claim that Spanish, for example, is not in the learner's world for a significant proportion of children in the United States. Indeed, given the demographics of contemporary U.S. society, one could offer a fairly compelling argument that Spanish, at least, is in fact very much a part of the learner's world (see Carrasquillo and Rodriguez 1996).

Despite the presence of considerable linguistic diversity in the population of the United States, many claim that foreign language education in the United States is deplorably unsuccessful. Simone (1993) argues that "despite the trends in internationalism and multiculturalism, most foreign language instruction at both the school and college level has not changed significantly in the past half century" (15). Reagan and Case (1996) articulate the belief of many educators and noneducators alike when they assert that there "can be little doubt that for the vast majority of students in the United States foreign language education has been a failure" and that our students "overwhelmingly remain monolingual" (97).

The shortcomings of foreign language education in the United States are reflected in a variety of other sources as well. The President's Commission on Foreign Language and International Studies, for example, suggested that "the nation was in serious trouble in terms of the second language competence of its citizenry" (Omaggio 1986, 10). In *Strength Through Wisdom* (1979), the commission concluded that "Americans' incompetence in foreign languages is nothing short of scandalous" (12). The evaluation offered years prior by Jacques Barzun (1954) seems to also describe the contemporary condition of foreign language education in the United States:

> [B]oys and girls "take" French or Spanish or German . . . for three, four, or five years before entering college, only to discover there that they cannot read, speak, or understand it. The word for this type of instruction is not "theoretical" but "hypothetical." Its principle is "*If* it were possible to learn a foreign language in the way I have been taught, I should now know that language." (119)

And although confident foreign language educators routinely argue that "monolingualism is curable," they nevertheless continue to struggle with the fact that despite their best efforts, monolingualism remains a plague not only for many of their charges, but also for American society in general (Simon 1980).

Moreover, there are blatantly conflicting messages regarding the value of foreign language education for our students. There are, for example, a considerable number of structural factors that work against our students as they attempt to become communicatively competent in another language (Reagan and Osborn 1998). We start instruction much too late in a student's academic career and then offer too few hours of exposure to reach fluency. And, as the New York State Board of Regents discovered when they recently attempted to increase the requirements of foreign language study for students, support for foreign language education is far from universal. After clamorous protest, the board repealed the requirement. 'I think it's a great shame,' [Regent]

Mr. Meyer said. 'There's a real question today in New York and in the country as to whether people believe any longer in the value of foreign language' (Hendrie 1997, 3).

As language educators, you have no doubt learned of the myriad of methodological approaches developed to improve our track record in regard to successful foreign language education. In fact, so much time in your preparation is dedicated to discovering the method or set of methods that will increase our success that fundamental questions are being overlooked. How students learn or acquire languages should likely be a secondary concern to where, or in which contexts, languages are learned (see Chick 1996).

In other words, perhaps the perceived failures of foreign language education in the United States are less related to methodological issues than they are to sociological issues. The issue of *foreignness* is, in an important way, both reflective of the problems of contemporary U.S. foreign language education and indicative of the conceptual and ideological confusion that exists both within and beyond the field. Educators continue to call virtually all non-English languages "foreign" on the one hand, yet on the other hand deny foreign language credit for, by way of example, American Sign Language (ASL), because it is widely used in the United States. Reagan (1997b) has posited that these distinctions "are often used to disguise personal, political, and ideological biases" (7).

Apple (1979) has expanded on this theme as well. Over two decades ago, he noted in regard to educational terms that

> the field [of curriculum] has a tendency to "disguise" relations between people as relations between things or abstractions. Hence, ethical issues such as the profoundly difficult problem concerning ways by which one person may seek to influence another are not usually treated as important considerations. It is here that the abstract categories that grow out of institutional life become quite serious. (134)

As the population of the United States in the twenty-first century becomes increasingly diverse linguistically, the category of *foreignness* grows quite serious indeed.

The 1990 census noted that 32 million people, or some 12% of the U.S. population, are from homes in which languages other than English are spoken, and projections indicate that by the year 2040 that number will have climbed to 98.7 million, or 28% of the population (Center for Applied Linguistics 1995). In fact, in some of the largest U.S. school districts today, the number of limited-English-proficient students already reaches one in three, and the numbers in smaller districts are growing daily (Fitzgerald 1993). The United States has, in short, become the most multilingual and multicultural nation on earth (Simone 1993).

Does the concept of *foreignness* serve to disguise relationships steeped in power inequalities between people as simply a categorical adjective? If we simply avoid the term "foreign," does that satisfy the demands of political correctness alone, all the while avoiding, or further disguising, the real issues? Language educators who are critically reflective should be able to answer such questions with reasonable confidence. Ethically, of course, we all need to answer those questions.

AN OVERVIEW OF RELEVANT RESEARCH

Scholars have addressed issues of social identity, language ownership and domination, language and ideology, and the possible impact of postmodernism in the field of language pedagogy (Benesch 1993; Kumaravadivelu 1994; Widdowson 1994). Peirce (1995) effectively contends that second language acquisition theorists have failed to consider important social aspects in the language learning context. Shanahan (1998) has questioned the oppositional assumptions language teachers make about culture and argues for a more universal approach to teaching cultural understanding. Otherwise, one can find reports of language education and inequality that are usually confined to bilingual education or English as a Second Language (ESL) programs, rather than foreign language classrooms (Darder 1991). Ricento (1998), in regard to bilingual education programs, has noted:

Policies that violate *deep values* will be difficult, if not impossible, to implement. Deep values represent an accretion of national experiences, influenced by certain intellectual traditions, which together create underlying, usually unstated or hegemonic frameworks within which policies evolve and are evaluated. . . . deep values refers to attitudes and beliefs about language and cultural (including national) identity. (89)

Power and Inequality in Language Education (Tollefson 1995), as well, is concerned with United States ESL and bilingual programs, and in-

cludes Auerbach's (1995) important treatment of the power of pedagogical decisions in the ESL classroom within the areas of curriculum
development, instructional content, materials, and language choice.
This excellent volume contains examinations of other language education programs in an international perspective.

A limited number of studies have also addressed the issue of the "culture" that exists within foreign language classrooms in the U.S. and
overseas. For example, Bromidge and Burch (1993) report that some
faculty have suggested that the foreign language classroom, especially
in regard to target language (L2), simulates the target culture. Students' attitudes about speaking the foreign language were shown to be
dependent on the extent to which their teachers used it during classroom instruction (Department of Education and Science 1990). One
study found that in Illinois secondary classes there was low use of the
target language by the teacher in first- and second-year foreign language courses (Connor 1995).

Van Meter (1990) asserts that ESL courses are not equivalent to
foreign language courses and thus giving college credit must be ap-
proached differently. Raphan and Gertner (1990) have contrasted the
pedagogical framework of ESL and foreign language classes in regard
to goals, student attitudes, backgrounds, motivations, and other cognitive and sociocultural factors. Swan (1985a, 1985b) has examined
the communicative approach from a critical perspective. Finally, Reagan and Osborn (1998) have called for an examination of the subculture of the classroom and Osborn and Reagan (1998) have argued
that this subculture may work against initiatives related to multicultural education.

WHY DOES ALL OF THIS MATTER?

In a liberal Western democratic society such as the United States, as
in most developed nations, the concept of equality in education is fundamental to educational praxis (Irwin 1996; Soder 1996). It is of great
concern, then, if any educational setting actively, even if unintention-
ally, somehow produces or reproduces forms of social inequality. In
terms of language education, if a course contributes to making all non-
English languages associated with that which is foreign, and then requires all college-bound students to pass through this educational environment as a filter to graduation from both secondary schools and
colleges, ideological frameworks are being developed in the minds of

members of the higher socioeconomic strata in society. Ideologically, language students are introduced to what it means to be "foreign."

Ideology has been defined as false consciousness (Marx 1972), as a set of beliefs that are nonscientific in nature (Althusser 1969), and as a set of beliefs that legitimize domination and repression (Habermas 1972). Giroux (1997b) has argued that ideology is a "set of beliefs and modes of discourse constructed to satisfy the needs and interests of specific groups" (73). McLaren (1989) posits that the term "refers to the production and representation of ideas, values, and beliefs and the manner in which they are expressed and lived out by both individuals and groups" (176), while Geuss (1981) points out that it is "the particular insidiousness of ideology that it turns human desires and aspirations against themselves and uses them to fuel repression" (88). Ideologically based elements of education, in turn, contribute to dominance and oppression by which one segment of the population, referred to as sharing the dominant culture, exerts its will over other segments of the society, without the use of force. This dominance is consented to by those oppressed segments, and the resultant process is referred to as *hegemony*.

Though equality in contemporary education is a laudable goal, given current practice it may be more mythological than actually attainable. The concept as used in the United States seems to represent an ideal, but most modern approaches to implement equity in education fail to address the fact that in reality the process of schooling is imbued with the values of the dominant class. These values are embedded in and become visible in discourse (see, for example, Gee 1996).

Fairclough (1989) notes that "orders of discourse, as dimensions of the social orders of social institutions or societies, are themselves shaped and constituted by relations of power" (43). Within the sphere of education, for example, textbooks, curriculum guides, and even the teachers themselves serve as examples of dominant discourse(s) insofar as they provide what the school legitimates as knowledge. Culture is also connected with social structures and can be analyzed as a form of production of social differences. It "is viewed as a field of struggle in which the production, legitimation, and circulation of particular forms of knowledge and experience are central areas of conflict" (McLaren 1989, 171).

As language teachers are aware, our instructional parameters include both grammatical items and cultural ones. It is within this framework that we must be exceptionally vigilant. The issues of power underlying the process of delimiting *foreignness* within the context of language education need to be fully investigated along with the impact such a concept may have in a broader social context, specifically the culture of the United States (see Davis 1990). If this impact includes a cultural component that may contribute to the marginalization of speakers of one or several languages, such a possibility must be evaluated with certain diligence. And finally, teachers must be empowered to make a difference in light of their renewed understanding.

THE LANGUAGE–CULTURE CONNECTION

A language policy perspective, or insight from the sociology of language related to education, typically includes recognition of the powerful nexus among language, identity, and culture. It is difficult to overstate the extent to which culture and language are intertwined. Some believe that languages determine one's *Weltanschauung*, or world-view, whereas others believe that language transmits culture. The Sapir-Whorf hypothesis takes the connection to the extent that the formulation of a thought in one language is considered to differ dramatically from the same process in a different language, thus making language the determinant of one's culture (see Cooper and Spolsky 1991). Other scholars have concluded that since languages have universal characteristics, such mutual exclusion does not exist; instead, they favor the idea of linguistic relativity. As Lucy (1996) clarifies,

> Any investigation of the relation between language and thought must also cope with this level of functional diversity in natural languages. The question is whether patterns of use have an impact on thought either directly or by virtue of amplifying or channeling any effects due to linguistic structure. We can call this the hypothesis of *discursive relativity*, a relativity stemming from diversity in the *functional* (or goal-oriented) configuration of language means in the course of (inter)action. (52)

Pool (1979) proposes that by changing one's language one thinks differently, to which Eastman (1983) adds that one would in some sense be changing his/her ethnic identity as a result of such a language shift. Littlewood (1981) concurs,

> When we try to adopt new speech patterns, we are to some extent
> giving up markers of our own identity in order to adopt those of
> another cultural group. In some respects, too, we are accepting
> another culture's ways of perceiving the world. If we are agreeable
> to this process, it can enrich us and liberate us. (55)

In terms of foreign language education, then, it is commonly held that
the experience of learning another language is beneficial inasmuch as it
enriches one's education by broadening one's potential *Weltanschauung*.

Occasionally, however, this broadening of one's *Weltanschauung* is
artificial and used for political ends. Such is the case when the difference
between being educated and uneducated is elevated and compared to
that between being a human being or not. And sadly, foreign language
education can be seen as part of the passage. As Gates (1992) explains:
Alexander Crummell, a pioneering nineteenth-century Pan-Africanist,
statesman, and missionary,

> shared with his audience a conversation between two Boston law-
> yers which he had overheard when he was "an errand boy in the
> Anti-slavery office in New York City" in 1833 or 1834: While at
> the capital they happened to dine in the company of the great
> John C. Calhoun, then senator from South Carolina. It was a pe-
> riod of great ferment upon the question of Slavery, States' Rights,
> and Nullification; and consequently the Negro was the topic of
> conversation at the table. One of the utterances of Mr. Calhoun
> was to this effect "That if he could find a Negro who knew the
> Greek syntax, he would then believe that the Negro was a human
> being and should be treated as a man." . . . Crummell himself
> jumped on a boat, sailed to England, and matriculated at Queens'
> College, Cambridge, where he mastered the intricacies of Greek
> syntax. (72–73)

Obviously, such an inflammatory definition of *human being* is absurd.
Nonetheless, the vignette serves as a reminder that learning a foreign
language has often been considered a prerequisite to being well educated or well rounded and has even been used to silence diverse voices.

However, classical Greek (or Spanish, French, German, Italian, etc.)
syntax is only one element of a foreign language curriculum. Because
language differs fundamentally as a subject, there is concomitant subject matter, namely, culture. As Kramsch (1993) explains,

One often reads in teachers' guidelines that language teaching consists of teaching the four skills [reading, writing, listening, and speaking] "plus culture." This dichotomy of language and culture is an entrenched feature of language teaching around the world. It is part of the linguistic heritage of the profession. Whether it is called (Fr.) *civilisation*, (G.) *Landeskunde*, or (Eng.) *culture*, culture is often seen as mere information conveyed by the language, not as a feature of language itself; cultural awareness becomes an educational objective in itself, separate from language. If however, language is seen as social practice, culture becomes the very core of language teaching. Cultural awareness must then be viewed both as enabling language proficiency and as being the outcome of reflection on language proficiency. (8)

Some scholars have even suggested that cultural knowledge should be considered as a priority over linguistic knowledge in the language classroom (see Byram and Morgan 1994; Lambert 1974). Yet Moore's (1996) research of foreign language classrooms supports the claim that culture is still treated in this context as a curricular "add-on," rather than an integral course component.

There is little consensus, however, on how effective cultural studies in a foreign language class could be in promoting linguistic equality or a cross-cultural understanding. Seelye (1974) claims: "One cannot understand a native speaker if his cultural referents, his view of the world, and his linguistic forms are novel. The language teacher can build bridges from one cognitive system to another" (22). Kramsch (1993), however, cautions again,

> What we should seek in cross-cultural education are less bridges than a deep understanding of the boundaries. We can teach the boundary, we cannot teach the bridge. We can *talk about* and try to *understand* the differences between the values celebrated in the American Coca-Cola commercial and the lack or the existence of analogous values in its Russian or German equivalents. We cannot teach directly how to resolve the conflict between the two. (228)

If language education carries inherent cultural messages, it also communicates something in relation to those people who use the language and are engaged in the cultural practices and beliefs associated with it. Brosh (1993) has even posited that a language learner's motivation to acquire a language may be directly influenced by its status in the larger sociological and sociopolitical environment. In referring to the study of Arabic in Israel, Brosh notes,

> Arabic is perceived as inherently connected to an ill-esteemed, dangerous, and hostile collective. As a result, the language is perceived as a marker of inferiority, and possessing it could be a source of negative gratification. (355)

Dicker (1996) asserts that there is no immunity to stereotyping people based on the language that they speak. Skutknabb-Kangas (1981) echoes this sentiment, explaining that the "language itself comes to constitute a symbolic representation of the group" (15). And Fishman (1991) agrees, noting that "[a]lmost all the languages of the world have also come to stand for the particular ethnic collectivities that speak them" (23).

The ties between language and culture and groups of people take on an enormous significance in terms of success and failure of the educational experience. As I have argued elsewhere,

> Mathematics teachers, for example, may play a determinant role in the attitude of their students toward math, and several teachers consciously attempt to prevent their students from developing "math anxiety." However, if a student has a bad experience in high school biology, s/he may well not like science for the remainder of life, though s/he had enjoyed it at an earlier time. S/he may think that frogs are disgusting, insects appalling, and botanical studies quite boring. S/he may even think that biologists are strange individuals. But it is quite likely that the experience will not translate into some sociologically relevant bias. This assurance is much weaker if one has a negative experience in a foreign language class. (Osborn 1997, 14)

Empirical studies have also attributed success (or failure) in this context as having a greater influence on attitudes than vice versa (Littlewood 1981; McDonough 1981).

In fact, the United States has seen its share of hostility between ethnic groups. The attempts to counter the trend through multicultural education have met both resistance and criticism (Corson 1989), and based on current trends in Official English movements (Dicker 1996), multicultural education initiatives cannot claim widespread acceptance of linguistic diversity as an accomplishment. To address this ongoing issue, other innovative approaches to incorporating foreign language and culturally relevant studies within the curriculum have emerged; again, though, with limited success evident (Connors 1984; Corson 1989; Maxim 1998; Wright and LaBar 1984).

Antonio Gramsci (1972) made a now often-quoted observation regarding the issue of language:

> Each time that, in one way or another, the question of language comes to the fore, that signifies that a series of other problems is about to emerge, the formation and enlarging of the ruling class, the necessity to establish more intimate and sure relations between the ruling groups and the national popular masses that is, the reorganization of cultural hegemony. (52)

Corson (1990) illuminates this issue at greater length, and is worth quoting in full:

> Obviously language is a key factor in reproducing and maintaining the features of cultures and societies, since a rich access to the dominant language gives individuals and groups power over their own affairs and influence over the affairs of others. As a result they are able to shape societies to serve their own ends and maintain them in the form to which they are accustomed. . . . [T]hose who control the conventions of discourse and who have the loudest voices most often have their interests promoted. At the same time those denied rich access to the dominant language and the power to make their own language more influential are hindered in expressing themselves, in drawing attention to their needs, and in commanding the support of others in the culture. (77)

Corson's claims can be extended to an argument about foreign language education in the United States as well. In a culturally pluralistic society such as the United States, those who do not speak the dominant language are certainly "hindered in expressing themselves, in drawing attention to their needs, and in commanding the support of others in the culture." If, however, those speaking the dominant language were also competent speakers/communicators of the nondominant languages, the hindrances Corson attributes to language would either be severely diminished or eliminated. The resultant empowerment of those who, in the United States, do not speak English as a native language would be unprecedented in recent history.

On the other hand, if native speakers of English are inculcated into ideological frameworks that define *foreignness* based on relative status of native languages, and exposure to the educational context within which the concept is reproduced becomes mandated for educational advancement, a more treacherous situation may result. Eastman (1983), drawing on Kelman (1971), provides an example of such a situation:

> People in high places in the educational and socioeconomic arenas who also have political power are IDEOLOGICALLY INTE-GRATED into the political context. That is, powerful, wealthy, educated people believe in what the system stands for. . . . The legitimacy of a political system depends on the ideological integration of elites. (149)

The integration of the elite, or even those who speak the same language as the elite, can be accomplished through education (see, for example, Apple 1988, 1993; Arnowitz and Giroux 1991; Freire 1985; Giroux 1983, 1988, 1991, 1993, 1997b; McLaren 1997, 1998). Yet neither the dominant language group nor the linguistic minority group may even be cognizant of the process in action:

> The members of some social groups, as a result, come to believe that their educational failure, rather than coming from their lowly esteemed social status, results from their natural inability. They come to believe that social and cultural factors are somehow neutralised in the educational selection process and that the process itself is fairly based on objective educational criteria, like possession of knowledge about the culture and the language necessary for expressing it.
>
> Language is the most important aspect of the cultural heritage that each of us receives and there is much evidence that "language" operates in a discriminatory way in educational settings. Apart from the obvious aspects of language, like its syntax, sounds and vocabulary, each of us acquires in our socialisation certain attitudes towards words and their use which we use to make judg-

ments about which forms of expression seem to us to be superior
to others. (Corson 1990, 223)

Darder (1991) notes that language domination involves a two-fold
process: stripping bicultural students of their native language and incul-
cating them into a belief system that supports the preeminence of English (see also Daniels 1990). However, McLaren (1989) is correct when
he identifies hegemony as "a cultural encasement of meaning, a prison
house of language and ideas that is *freely entered in both by dominators
and dominated*" (124, italics added). Language domination, at least in
the context of the United States, must include a third element of promoting or obtaining the buy-in of the dominant language group.[4]
Analyzing the ways in which foreign language education in the United
States delimits *foreignness* will aid in understanding of this "side of the
coin" (see also Beyer and Apple 1988; Giroux 1997a; Kress and Hodge,
1979; Macedo 1994; Milroy and Milroy, 1985). This understanding is
especially vital since it is through this context, our context of the foreign language classroom, that virtually all college-bound students and
college graduates must come.

CONCLUSION

In this chapter, I have introduced language teachers to the broad
range of issues that have typically been absent from their professional
preparation. I have attempted to raise in your mind the possibility that
the foreign language classroom is not simply an environment in which
neutral vocabulary and grammatical structures are taught. It is my intention that you understand that the foreign language classroom is a
site of cultural struggle. And whether we like it or not, we are participants in the struggle. As such, it is time that this awareness becomes
part of the teacher's preparation and ongoing professional development, and that we move beyond methodology.

If the terms and concepts presented in this chapter seem to be yet another "foreign" language to you, the reader, let me encourage you
again to be patient. It will take some time to develop a critical *Sprachge-
fühl*, but it will be of significant impact on the lives of your students. It has
the potential to make language teaching "alive" in ways we have yet to
imagine.

In the following chapters, the discussion will focus on developing insights and skills as a critically reflective language educator by examining

the principles and practices of United States foreign language education, including curricular mandates and presentations, as well as the larger social context within which these elements operate. Though in this chapter much attention has been focused on the voices of scholars, in subsequent ones the intent is to assist you, the language teacher, in finding your own critically reflective voice. Chapter Two explores more in depth the connections between language education and cultural struggle, including examples from around the world. Chapter Three focuses on the nature of critical educational studies and the language of critical pedagogy. Chapter Four examines the process of critical reflection by moving outside the foreign language classroom and analyzing evidence of cultural struggle in education along with the possibilities of reform. Chapter Five leads students through the process of seeing the concept of *foreignness* as it is found in textbooks and curriculum guides, with implications for practice. In Chapter Six the reader will develop approaches for creating a more critical "foreign" language classroom, exploring the topics of curricular nullification, authentic empowerment, interdisciplinary activities, and community-based learning. Finally, Chapter Seven anticipates the vision of a new professional language educator, including bridging the now separate "disciplines" of foreign language education and English as a second language or bilingual education.

QUESTIONS FOR DISCUSSION

How has your own education in language addressed (or failed to address) the ways in which language operates in society?

How does language education act as a filter for who gains access to certain places or roles in society?

Describe how you think U.S.-Americans perceive non-English languages. Can you provide examples to support your view?

NOTES

1. *Webster's Encyclopedic Unabridged Dictionary of the English Language,* 1996.

2. It should be noted at this point that English does enjoy the status of official language at the state level in several instances.

3. By this term I intend to contrast "structural monolingualism" with a legislatively determined monolingualism or other explicit language policy. Monolingualism, though perhaps *de facto*, is not neutrally determined when

societal structures, organization(s), and so on provide overwhelming support to the one language at the same time actively discouraging the broad acceptance of nondominant languages.

4. In order for language domination to be hegemonic, the dominant class as well must be inculcated into the ideology that supports those ends. Native and non-native speakers alike must come to believe that English is superior in the society. For both, *foreignness* as discussed in this text can be seen as part of that process.

Chapter 2

Language Education and Culture

If one were to ask ten educators to define culture, a minimum of eleven proposed definitions would likely result. Culture, for both language educators and others, is difficult to pin down as to what precisely is being described. Lessow-Hurley (1996) has pointed out that

> Culture is something we all have but often find difficult to perceive. Culture, like language, is dynamic, changing to meet the needs of the people it serves. All cultures have coherent, shared systems of action and belief that allow people to function and survive. (95)

Goodman (1992), on the other hand, points to culture as the "learned, socially transmitted heritage of artifacts, knowledge, beliefs, values and normative expectations that provides the members of a particular society with the tools for coping with recurrent problems" (338). Shanahan (1998), instead of providing an oversimplified definition, argues that there are five "major approaches to the notion of culture with relevance for foreign language teaching" (451), while Mayer (1993) stresses that

[A]nthropologists have long recognized that studying the language of a culture is essential to understanding it, and in some ways the two cannot be meaningfully separated since so many of a culture's assumptions and practices are embedded in and revealed by the particulars of its language system. (564)

For the purposes of this text, it is perhaps best to speak of culture as a concept. Two conceptualizations of culture should already be familiar to foreign or world language educators,[1] and usually we refer to them as capital "Culture" (or sometimes "high culture") and lowercase "c" culture (or "low culture"). But world language educators should also be familiar with two other concepts of culture: what I have decided to call classroom culture, and culture as a commodity. In this chapter, we will discuss at length the connections between language education and culture with a goal of heightening your awareness of cultural struggles existing both in language and education. Specifically, you will be challenged to reject the notion that the foreign language classroom is devoid of political, or power-imbued, activity. In other words, all four concepts of culture have underlying power relationships, most often disguised, that have an impact on students' thinking and, as a result, their lives and the lives of their neighbors.

QUESTIONS FOR REFLECTION

How has culture typically been defined in the language classes you have taken?

How would you define or describe your own culture?

CAPITAL "C" CULTURE

The works of Cervantes, Goethe, Molière, and Dante are typically heralded as the greats of literature. The contributions of Bach, Beethoven, Brahms, as well as Louis Pasteur, Van Gogh, and Michelangelo are certainly worthy of note in a course that teaches their respective languages. But let us consider how in contemporary society these unique individuals have become part of "high culture."

Pointing to what is commonly described as the canon, scholars have challenged the assumption that one can neutrally define a set of literary works that are inherently meritorious. The selection of the "great works" reflects a segment of the population who, threatened both by these [contemporary] demographic shifts and by the demand for curricular change, has retreated to a stance of intellectual protectionism, arguing for a great and inviolable "western tradition" which contains the seeds, fruit, and flowers of the very best that has been thought or uttered in human history. (Gates 1992, 174)

Such appeals to what Schubert (1996) refers to as intellectual tradition-alism are, in fact, rooted in cultural struggle. Yet these struggles are rarely included in any delineation of the foreign language canon.

The purpose here is not to dismiss the contributions of the "greats." Instead, world language educators need to understand that there are no natural and neutral criteria for evaluating works of art, literature, or even science that make these contributors to *Culture* worthy of inclusion. Instead, it is because of the decisions of primarily academics and business*men* that these works continue to take their place among recommended and required reading.

The issue of scientific contributions seems to be odd to include in this list, perhaps. But even the scientific world has entertained skirmishes based on other than "scientific" bases. In reference to the warnings of Carl Sagan and others about the dangers of nuclear winter, for example, Dyson (1988) explains that

nuclear winter is not just a theory. It is also a political statement with profound moral implications. . . . So my instinct as a scientist comes into sharp conflict with my instinct as a human being. As a scientist I want to rip the theory of nuclear winter apart, but as a human being I want to believe it. (259)

Thus, as one decides which scientists' achievements are worthy of note in a language course, which implications take precedence: theoretical, political, moral, or others?

The issue for language courses is two-fold: first, whose works, and therefore voices, are not being heard by our students because they fail to meet these inherently biased standards of "greatness," and second, what impression are we leaving with students about the neutrality of the selection process? Are native speakers of the language in the United States who write, as it were, in exile from the "foreign" countries, given opportunities to become part of the literary canon? And if not, how can our students hear the voices of even their own neighbors in, for example, literature and art?

QUESTIONS FOR REFLECTION

Have you questioned the value of works you read in your language and literature classes that you thought were not really impressive? Did you or others voice your doubts? What response did you receive?

Can you name authors, painters, poets, or others whose works are deserving of attention, but who have received little praise? Do you know of any in the United States?

What kind of topics or themes do you think are less likely to be found in language textbook literary selections? Why?

LOWERCASE "C" CULTURE

What kind of greetings do speakers of a language give each other: a handshake, a kiss on the cheek, a hug? When invited to dinner, what kind of gift should one bring along? How many days of the week do speakers of the language in other countries go to school? These are many of the questions that can be asked and answered in a discussion of *culture*. And similar to *Culture*, these items are not neutral or natural, but based on a social context.

The Germans often bring a *Mitbringsel*, typically flowers, when invited to a meal at someone's house. Italian-Americans, likewise, may bring pastries—cannoli are usually a good choice. These cultural practices become part of a fabric of everyday life so much that most native speakers of the language neither question nor at times even understand them. Language students, on the other hand, for whom such practices differ from their own, are usually introduced to them through cultural blurbs in textbook chapters, usually in the form of a paragraph or two in some corner of the chapter.

We need to be aware, however, of (1) how the information is presented, that is, as chunks of virtual trivia to be stored away, and (2) how, for example, forms of etiquette are represented without regard to power relationships underlying the socially constructed meaning. Let us turn to the latter issue first.

Etiquette, or any form of social grace, tends to represent to other members of a culture a certain level of education or even "refinement." Usually, though, the fork to use for salad versus the one for seafood rarely is discussed in the language class. Instead, we present information on, for example, formal versus familiar forms of address (tú, Usted; du, Sie; and so on). These distinctions are important for our students to know, particularly in regard to how they will be perceived by native speakers of the language. But the distinctions are neither neutral nor natural. They are constructed both socially and historically to have symbolic meaning. And their usage, as a result, conveys social and symbolic messages about both speaker and hearer. How clumsy is the American who uses the wrong form of address for, by way of example, a mature woman or a dog? How is that person likely to be perceived?

One of my students learned this lesson the hard way. As he entered the store in a small, psuedo-alpine village in northeast Georgia, he was anxious to try out his German. Though I had stressed the importance of using the formal form of address, he was accustomed to the familiar form in his practice with fellow students. He addressed the matronly German-speaking shop owner in the familiar, and received a stern lecture that I imagine he remembers to this day.

Yet, most often, our students are not likely to actually practice the kind of etiquette taught in foreign language classes, nor even discuss holidays, school routines, or anything else we teach as *culture*, since they are rarely called upon to interact with citizens of the "foreign" countries. Instead, their interactions with speakers of non-English languages are more likely to take place in the United States. Therefore, the validity of a claim that all of this information is necessary for our students to use the language is, at least, suspect. However, since the information as presented most often highlights differences from the students' own practices, the cultural referents tend to take on a feel of novelty. And sadly, often teachers report that the texts even get the *culture* information wrong.

Students begin to build a conceptual framework in this way of how the target culture's practices are different from, for lack of a better expression, "mainstream" U.S.-American practices. These chunks of knowledge, reflecting what Freire has called a banking model of education, contribute to another cultural referent in the United States society, that is, *foreignness*. Though we will discuss this concept in greater detail in future chapters, two examples are in order at this time.

One textbook attempts to assist students in understanding that time is a culturally framed referent:

In general, North Americans have a different concept of time than do Latin Americans. In Latin American countries, it is acceptable to arrive at social events well after the appointed time. When invited to dinner, people from Spanish-speaking countries might ask if the time is *hora americana* or *hora latina* in order to know whether or not to be punctual. In contrast, Spanish speakers are generally punctual when they go to work or to school. Which attitude toward time—the North American or the Latin American—makes you feel more comfortable? (Jarvis et al. 1989, 49)

Among other problems, to question students as to what makes them feel comfortable seems to invite the comparison of uncomfortable feelings in regard to one of the two attitudes. Perhaps even more critical, however, is that this bifurcation of time referents reinforces another referent, *foreignness*. The phrases *hora americana* and *hora latina* seem to indicate that one way of viewing time is inherently American whereas another is Latin. Though the distinction is based on Spanish linguistic content, the text's question about North American versus Latin American attitudes contributes to a conceptualization of *foreignness* in lower-case "c" culture.

A second example follows a similar line of logic:

Look at the following photographs [of people either shaking hands, holding hands, or kissing as in greeting or leave-taking]. From the actions of the people, do you think the people are from an Hispanic country or from the United States? Tell why. (Woodford, Schmitt, and Marshall 1989, 119)

This exercise not only reinforces the idea that you can tell differences in nationality on sight, but also assumes that Americans could not follow "Hispanic" customs in regard to greeting or leave-taking. As a result, students who leave the foreign language classroom and see Latinos or others in their own towns who practice such behaviors might perceive those citizens as foreign.

The *culture* as presented in these examples is given a comparative and contrastive context, but the examples reveal disturbing assumptions about what is considered "American"[2] and what is considered "foreign." Those categories, however, feed into cultural struggles within and beyond the classroom.

QUESTIONS FOR REFLECTION

What did you learn in your language classes about "typical" behavior of speakers of the language?

Can comparison and contrast in instruction avoid setting up categories of "us" and "them?" If so, how? If not, why not?

CLASSROOM CULTURE

Because language classes can vary so dramatically in terms of content and even behavior patterns, it is at least problematic to discuss them as a culture. Some might suggest that they are, at best, subcultures, perhaps even countercultures, and most would agree that they reflect elements of a broader culture. All of these claims are, to a point, true. Nonetheless, I have chosen to refer to the language classroom as a culture because there are elements within it that are quite unique to this context. These elements also, sometimes significantly, contain elements of cultural struggle.

Though most students enter a mathematics or literature class with some limited knowledge of the subject, it is not at all uncommon for students to walk into a foreign language classroom with virtually no background knowledge in the subject of their study. Naturally disoriented by their virtually complete inability to communicate in the target language, these students encounter the foreign language teacher and are led or guided, hopefully, to a new set of skills, a new route of personal expression. Due to the intimate nature of this expression, the foreign language class can have fundamentally beneficial, or detrimental, effects on the student.

Foreign language teachers share a certain culture as well. Dealing with students can be a most frustrating part of a language teacher's job. Foreign languages are not the most popular of subjects and current methodological trends favor relaxed environments where students are free to express themselves in meaningful ways (Richards and Rodgers 1986). At the same time, however, foreign language teachers are often non-native speakers themselves, and thus face a feeling of anxiety as they approach their linguistic task (Horwitz 1996). Thus, dealing with behavioral issues becomes of prime importance for the language teacher.

In qualitative-based studies,[3] I have attempted to explore this issue of a "foreign language education culture." As one language teacher expressed it, "We are a tight group. It is the nature of language teaching.

A language is alive and well, there is a dynamic that is a group dynamic."
Another teacher saw it similarly:

> We are different [from others]. There is a sensibility, an apprecia-
> tion of global things. We are less practical. We like the richness and
> experience that comes from languages. There is lots of personality.
> Students perceive foreign language teachers as different. My hus-
> band, a math teacher, says we are different. Others think we must
> be freaks since we speak different languages. We must be "super-
> brainy."

When I asked students if foreign language teachers were different from
their other teachers, one group of seniors gave overwhelming support
to the idea:

1. Yes, because they give more personal attention and receive more
   class participation.
2. Yes, they're a lot easier to work with. They keep taking into account
   that the subject isn't natural as are other subjects to us.
3. [Y]ou usually have them more than one year so you have a chance to
   get to know you [*sic*] better . . . a little more interested in their students than regular teachers.
4. They're completely happy, pleasant, friendly, and a little on the exotic side. They're completely open with you, and down to earth.
   They're nicer and funer [*sic*]. The class itself is pleasant and positive,
   whereas in other classes you tend to feel negative and put down. Language teachers are very encouraging. They believe in everyone.
5. Yes, they are a bit looney.

Whether "looney" or happy, most language teachers I have encoun-
tered are convinced they are performing a valuable service for their students. They are introducing them to a world broader, yet smaller, than
the students had ever imagined.

Yet at the secondary level, most students are usually "tracked" into
either college preparatory or vocational preparatory programs, with
some systems still having a general track; typically these consist of a
combination of the college preparatory and vocational programs.
Common to each college preparatory program is the requisite two
years of coursework in the same language.

The foreign language teacher is thus placed in the position of deciding (along with other faculty) who will receive the college endorsement on their diplomas. Although other requirements exist, foreign language departments tend to be small, and as a result students often have little or no choice as to who their instructor will be for a given language and level. Given the two years continuity requirement, switching languages can be exceedingly difficult. From my own experience, I have known teachers who were, and have been myself, the sole reason a student did not receive the college preparatory endorsement. Certainly, I would claim that the student's course performance was the actual reason, and to a point, that may be correct.

The native speaker of the foreign language must also meet the two-year foreign language requirement. Typically, the student is placed in a foreign language class in her or his own native language. In this absurd situation, I have known students to rely on their own knowledge rather than to study for tests, and some teachers who would not accept answers that, though correct, were not the "book answer." As an example, a student who spoke Spanish as his native language was placed in an introductory Spanish class and received no credit for a vocabulary quiz item because he wrote down the Puerto Rican expression, not the Castilian one. In another situation, native speakers of Spanish were enrolled in French classes en masse, reportedly to avoid the potential problems the students might have (and might pose) if enrolled in a course on their own language. Since foreign language teachers often replace guidance counselors in the context of placement adviser, some have been known to use this power to guide native speakers into an independent study course, thus isolating the native student and shielding the teacher from any classroom challenge to her/his own linguistic autonomy and authority.

In terms of course content, there has been a well-documented movement in the past twenty years or so away from "canned" expressions and sentences being used in the foreign language classroom, toward more authentic communication and a utilization of realia. Textbooks have been designed to focus on patterns of discourse that one might find in the target culture, typically including behavior such as buying vegetables, discussing hobbies or school activities, and careers. Unfortunately, however, these discussions are typically no more meaningful to our students than the contrived dialogues of audiolingualism or the tiresome translation of grammatical minutiae common in foreign language classes of the past. Despite the best intentions of language teachers, most of our students will never buy vegetables in a Munich street market, ask for directions to the Eiffel Tower in Paris, or have a school schedule in Mexico City. This being the case, it should not be particularly surprising to find that "foreign" language classrooms remain foreign to most of our students. And though some teachers attempt to spark interest by bringing their classes together in an interschool competition of foreign language skills (the items being tested including recitation of a poem, communication skills, and cultural information), for example, the trade-off in terms of student perception may range from seeing non-native languages as a potential competitive threat to trivializing the possession of second language skills.

This shift in pedagogical emphasis has had the effect of making the teacher increasingly the cultural authority within the classroom. Teachers decide which cultural information should be highlighted, which country should be highlighted, and which information is essential. Teachers quite naturally tend to rely on information from cultures with which they are familiar (in the case of a German teacher, for example, this may mean Germany over Switzerland), and the interests or backgrounds of particular students could be subjugated. Moreover, textbook authors who attempt to provide a balanced view of various target cultures can be easily overridden, when a teacher simply chooses not to cover "that part of the chapter."

Another effect of curricular and methodological changes during the past half century has been the reorientation of course content in hopes of strengthening instruction, and educators now speak of developing *communicative competence*. In practice, though, this term has become virtually meaningless, as one can encounter at least three distinct uses for the term. First, it implies the development of a set of skills making one able to communicate in a second language "competently." This is the manner in which the term is primarily used in research literature. Second, the term *communicative competence* implies a goal of classroom instruction used by planners to describe a design that will hopefully enable, though not guarantee, students to possess certain skills in a classroom setting. Finally, the term functions as a slogan employed by researchers, classroom practitioners, or planners who may or may not be concerned with the skills previously mentioned. Stone (1990) refers to this phenomenon when he states that "communicative competence became the yardstick with which to beat those who taught in accordance with the old line-by-line translation methodology" (18). Those teachers may be using the term only in a general sense to mean de-emphasizing grammar in the classroom.

Within the framework of communicative competence, however, one also finds huge variation in regard to the issue of grammatical accuracy. Teachers who strive to develop communicative competence vary widely in their demands for grammatical accuracy. Some instructors believe that getting the idea across is enough, others demand that the idea be communicated such that a native who is not a teacher and knows no English would understand. Indeed, some may be even stricter. Due to the wide variations in this classroom goal, the teacher alone determines what is acceptable accuracy and what is not.

The level and frequency of usage of grammatical terminology is another element of course content that forms the foundation of a classroom culture. Students, native speakers and non-native speakers alike, tend to be largely unaware of the technical aspects of grammar, including the parts of speech or various elements of syntax. Some teachers typically have a sense of frustration at the students' lack of preparation in this area, and more recently I have heard discussion among experienced instructors that new teachers are ill-prepared to teach grammatical concepts. Discussing language primarily in terms of grammatical content continues to be a controversial practice in contemporary U.S. foreign language courses, but it still occurs with great frequency, often clearly in contradiction to contemporary methodological thought.

One final note on elements of course content is the "official code switch." Teachers dictate when classroom conversation should be in English or the foreign language and some have been known to ignore students speaking in the "wrong" language. Others even go to the extent of fining students for using the prohibited language (typically English). And since administrators rarely possess the skills in a foreign language to assess a teacher's proficiency, some teachers have been known to use code-switching as a strategy to increase the difficulty an administrator may have when observing a lesson. The hope is, as I have heard it expressed, that observers will assume since they hear a foreign language, sound instruction must be taking place.

The "culture" of a foreign language classroom is not different from that of other subjects in many ways.[4] The teacher is the "sage on the stage" in many courses. However, the subject matter being presented does differ in terms of its sociological nature. Language is a marker of identity, an expression of culture ("big C," "little c," and others), and a vehicle of personal expression in a way that biology or physical education are not. Even art, with its embodiment of a high level of personal expression, does not act as an evident and ready-made identifier of large segments of the population in the way a language does.

Moreover, the students are given the impression that in regard to language there is a "correct" form that is static. It is quite rare to find a teacher explaining to students the evolution of languages over time. The other curricular mandates simply do not allow time for any in-depth analysis, and most teachers are probably grossly unaware of the particulars of language change.

Tragically, by failing to address the sociological nature of language in both its nature and use, the foreign language classroom reinforces the myths surrounding the standard or "correct" form of all languages, especially English in the United States. Moreover, we fail to alert students that these distinctions are primarily political, not linguistic. As Lippi-Green (1997) states so well with regard to English,

> What our schools do, for the most part, is to insist that some children forego the expressive power and consolation of speech in that variety of English which is the currency of their home communities. This gesture of denial and symbolic subordination is projected as a first and necessary step to becoming a good student and a good citizen. (132)

If even varieties of English are subjected to this symbolic subordination, then certainly non-English languages used in the United States suffer a similar fate.

As noted in the discussion of the culture of the foreign language classroom, secondary teachers have not, to date, had the space to bring to the attention of the college-bound populace an awareness of these issues. As a result, it would seem, the majority of Americans have little understanding of the language issues that affect their, and their nation's, everyday lives. As Coleman (1996) points out,

> In some situations, the language classroom may be the context for the learning of other things in addition to—or even in the place of—language. . . . If this hypothesis is confirmed, then, of course, innovation in classroom methodology may have unexpected repercussions for the teaching/learning of these "other things." Al-

ternatively, if these issues are not taken into consideration, then innovations in classroom practice may be taking on some unexpected functions even when they do apparently take root. (10–11)

These "other things" can be traced as one begins to appreciate the role that foreign language education occupies in a larger societal context.

QUESTIONS FOR REFLECTION

How do foreign language classrooms function as a "culture"? What is unique about the context, the behaviors, the values, and so on?

Since students come to class with cultural backgrounds, how are their cultures treated or addressed within the "foreign language classroom culture"?

CULTURE AS COMMODITY—THE FOREIGN LANGUAGE CLASS EXPERIENCE

A common metaphor used in describing contemporary language education is that of building bridges of understanding between cultures. It is certainly a pleasing depiction, especially given the increasing diversity in the United States, but in actuality aspects of language education may contribute to the maintenance of cultural divides. The lack of appropriate time commitments coupled with generally accepted, but time-dependent, potential advantages of language study interact with an institutionally provided conceptualization of "otherness" I refer to as *foreignness* to cause this educational context to appear progressive interculturally, all the while perpetuating the very misconceptions it could, in fact, ameliorate.

Benefits of foreign language study usually cited by educators are directly tied to economic or status gain for members of the dominant language group. Examples often include increasing one's attractiveness to a prospective employer, fulfilling a prerequisite of college admission, and even the ability to compete in a global marketplace. Curricula as well customarily mention the significance of foreign language education in increasing students' awareness or acceptance of cultural and linguistic diversity. Routinely coupled with other humanistic advantages, foreign language education is presented as the near-panacea for cross-cultural or intercultural conflict based on advantages gained by students who, according to the newest foreign language learning standards and curricula, compare and contrast cultural influences on the lives of U.S. citizens. Consistently absent from this part of the discussions, however, is the role that achieved language skill plays in fostering these desired positive attitudes.

As a comparative example, though mathematics education certainly provides some benefits for daily life, few would argue that awareness of numbers alone results in true understanding. It is, in fact, the ability to apply and use those concepts in meaningful ways on a regular basis that is the greatest benefit provided by mathematics. Similarly, an awareness of cultural differences, without a concomitant linguistic skill, could result only in what Kramsch (1993) described as defining boundaries. The absence of such a qualification of the proposed "benefits" of foreign language study in terms of linguistic competence obscures the relative effectiveness of any instructional program in delivering the multiple benefits promised, and clouds the likely results of limited language study. In other words, it is likely that without the ability to actually communicate with members of the cultures represented by the languages of study, only an increased awareness results, not a multicultural acceptance based on experience.

Diagrammatically, one can understand both the proposed and actual benefits of foreign language study as ranging about two intersecting continua. Advantages can range from a personal good to a common good, from requiring little "foreign" linguistic skill to requiring considerable linguistic skill. If one were to then chart the advantages proposed by typical curricula on this diagram, with reference to relative linguistic skill required, the result(s) would be as depicted in Figure 1. As shown, the memorization of a plethora of grammatical rules, for example, may well result in enhanced study skills but will not result in the proficiency needed for tangible economic benefits related to proficiency.

Thus, the benefits of foreign language study that are related to employment enhancement are shown to require considerable linguistic skill to actually be credibly attributed to language education. And in any case, the promises of increased marketability are decidedly weak, as foreign language professionals admit: "As for studying a foreign language for vocational purposes, within this country there is almost always a plethora of native speakers of any language needed in commerce" (Idaho State Department of Education 1994, 21).

Within the foreign language class, a conceptualization of what can be termed *foreignness* is presented to students in multiple ways. Briefly

Figure 1
Proposed Curricular Advantages in Terms of Linguistic Skill Requirements

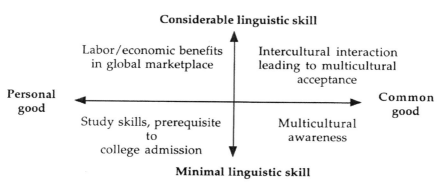

now let us consider the examples of geographic fragmentation, English language/American synonymy, language variety bias, and paternalistic empowerment.

When a foreign language teacher plans a lesson he or she often includes information about the country or countries where the target language is spoken. Furthermore, cultural information in terms of both social routines and major accomplishments in the arts, for examples, are regularly featured. Textbooks support this process by providing maps and cultural blurbs and by pointing out significant cultural elements. However, when the instructional focus turns to speakers of the language in the United States, one begins to detect inconsistencies in the portrayals. One of the most conspicuous examples of these dissimilarities can be seen in maps.

In French, German, and Spanish textbooks, a map usually found in the front pages points to the French-, German-, and Spanish-speaking world. For the *mundo hispánico*, Spain, Puerto Rico, and most of the countries of Central and South America are depicted in a highlighted color. The continental United States, however, is routinely either not highlighted, or only portions are noted: most commonly the states of California, New Mexico, Arizona, Texas, and Florida and the cities of New York and Chicago. In French textbooks, a similar pattern develops, with Louisiana and New England as the areas of the United States that are sometimes highlighted. In German and Russian textbooks, though, rarely is anything in the United States highlighted.

Though arguably such depictions are not blatantly inaccurate, they are certainly misleading. By appearing to limit linguistic diversity to certain geographical areas in the United States, and failing to carve analogous "holes" in countries where pockets of, for example, indigenous language speakers may live, the foreign language textbooks seem to fragment the United States alone into areas of significant linguistic diversity (e.g., part of the *mundo hispánico*). Further, by ignoring the linguistic diversity found in every area of the United States, the impact may be even more significant, since native speakers of Spanish or other non-English languages who live in nonhighlighted areas (Washington, DC, and Hartford, CT, for example), would appear to be the proverbial outsiders within.

It should be noted that geographic fragmentation is effective, only if "foreign" linguistic skills are impoverished. If all English-speaking Americans were successfully educated to be bilingual, geographical fragmentation would be meaningless in terms of where a "foreign" language is spoken in the United States. As it stands, however, the concept is inaccurate, but it provides an effective image of *foreignness* if most English-speaking Americans remain monolingual. The implications of such a concept in the classrooms of diverse urban environments should be especially disturbing.

The most pervasive indication of a conceptualization of *foreignness* found in the foreign language classroom seems to be a synonymy set up between the classification "American" and the English language. As a result, logically, non-English utterances could seem, somehow, un-American: "A student of Arabic might come to understand that the terms for *host* and *guest* imply more social obligations in the Middle East than they do in the United States" (California Department of Education 1989, 5). This claim is correct only if no one speaks Arabic in the United States. The social obligations are connected to the language in the first part of the claim. The second part of the claim, then, ties the language to a national identity. The implication is that the terms *host* and *guest* culturally cannot be part of the United States, if they are communicated in Arabic. Yet it is indeed the language that communicates the cultural connotation, not the nationality (unless assimilation is universal).

The English language/American synonymy as well is dependent on a broad-based failure of foreign language education programs to produce competent bilinguals or multilinguals. If all Americans were bilingual, this synonymy would be archaic. As long as monolingualism is "curable," that is, not "cured," then these embedded conflicts carry ideological weight and power, supported in commonsense linguistic assumptions of the world in which many U.S. citizens live.

An additional illustration of a way in which foreign language curricular documents and classroom activities contribute to the conceptualization of *foreignness* is related to the issue of language variety. Though linguists have noted that the differences between a language and a dialect are primarily political (Lippi-Green 1997), whether one is speaker of *Hochdeutsch* or Parisian French, foreign language classes tend to favor one language or language variety over others.

As one textbook addressed the issue of diglossia directly, in doing so it established the "superiority" of English:

> As we have said earlier, many Hispanic students already speak Spanish; however, it may not be the variety of language that is taught in the typical classroom. In sociolinguistic terms, people in this group are termed diglossic. This means that while one language is used for all formal or what are termed "high" functions, the other is used in all informal or "low" functions. In the case of the United States, English is generally considered appropriate for formal exchanges . . . and Spanish is used in informal situations within the home and among other members of the speech community. (Gutiérrez, Rosser, and Rosso-O'Laughlin 1997, 20)

Intriguingly, the authors note that sermons may serve as examples of formal language functions, but certainly within an urban environment religious services in all faiths are commonly carried out in non-English languages. The discussion seems, on the whole, to be an attempt first, to help teachers understand what a Spanish class can offer a native speaker, and second, to correct the myth of dialect meaning "substandard language." Nonetheless, it is certainly the case that all language varieties are not considered equal in the foreign language class.

Finally, many foreign language curricula speak in glowing terms of the results for speakers of the "foreign language" when speakers of English learn another language. The resultant description of a paternalistic, and therefore false, empowerment or validation is likewise a most effective image when students possess minimal language skills. Consider the following example:

Students without a hearing impairment may enroll in those [ASL] classes. When they do, the state's hearing-impaired students become less isolated from the social and economic mainstream. Their confidence and self-esteem increase. (California Department of Education 1989, 12)

Regardless of how well-intentioned they might be, such comments are deeply embedded in a deficit/deficiency view of the non-native speaker of English as needing assistance or validation from the dominant language group.

Yet if most Americans were bilingual, though equality of language status still might not be realized, a relative equality in the accessibility to power of speakers of all non-English languages would provide a structure which supports true self-empowerment. In other words, the status quo would not prevent such equal access simply by supporting a structural form of monolingualism, with the single language being English.

At this point, then, it is helpful to return to the figure of intersecting continua, but it is necessary to rename the ends of the horizontal axis as "individual focus" and "collective focus," since I am no longer describing only proposed benefits. As depicted in Figure 2, the possible outcomes of the "embedded conflicts" are also affected by relative linguistic skill or proficiency.

In short, for the contemporarily heralded goals of foreign language education to be realized, specifically those of making cross-cultural

Figure 2
Embedded Conflicts in Reference to Linguistic Skill Achievement

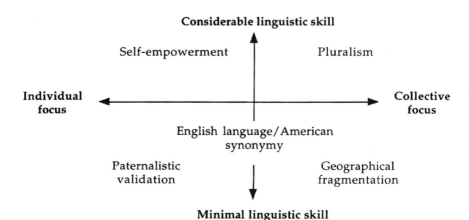

connections and a linguistically pluralistic society that is less imbued with power inequalities related to language, students in these classes would need, at a minimum, to reach levels of linguistic proficiency far beyond what the standard two-year requirement makes possible. Thus, Coleman's cautionary statement regarding "other things" becomes most germane. What is being learned in the foreign language class-rooms of the United States and, more to the point, which cultural struggles are going unrecognized? Answering these questions goes to the heart of critical reflection.

Consider that every student walks into a classroom with a background of interests, values, ways of speaking, dressing, and acting that are valued by those who are similar to them. This form of culture varies and has been the root of misunderstandings in the educational setting, specifi-cally as it relates to speakers of non-English languages (Carrasquillo and Rodriguez 1996). In certain regions of the country, adding "sir" or "ma'am" to the response to a question by an elder is a sign of respect, and is thought to indicate, at a certain level, the quality of one's upbringing. But absence of these expressions in those who are from outside that re-gion does not equate with disrespect. Likewise, when a person is ad-dressed by one in authority, in some cultures it is respectful to maintain eye contact with the speaker, while in others it is quite offensive.

The schools, despite perhaps the best intentions of some, are not neutral in regard to these cultural differences. Some differences are val-ued, some are not. In the United States, for example, students who are talkative in the classroom regarding the subject matter at hand are generally viewed as active, engaged learners. The aspect of many grades known as "class participation" is often designed to reward such appro-priate behavior. But this convention is grounded in those behaviors valued by the educators in this time and in this society. As a result, stu-dents whose cultural background might not reflect the same values may suffer in terms of evaluation of their academic performance. Lower grades may mean fewer opportunities for college admission or in the corporate world.

At the same time, some experiences, values, and behaviors are con-sidered valuable and expected in the places of privilege in society. At formal dinners, certainly, the multitude of forks beside one's plate are not interchangeable socially (though functionally, perhaps they are) and the guest who knows no difference will likely be noticed. Though a faux pas may not result in grievous discrimination, systematic devaluation of certain cultural expressions does, and it is this phenomenon that is of concern to those determined to teach with an orientation toward social justice and equity.

What does this have to do with foreign language education? Given that foreign language education is prerequisite to most college admissions, and secondary and tertiary graduations, and yet realistic expectations of proficiency are virtually nonexistent, then perhaps those who are successful in navigating the course requirements are actually only expected to understand the sentiment expressed in the statement, "Yeah, I took foreign languages in school, but I didn't learn anything." Moreover, even if the student cannot name what it is s/he learned, there is little possibility that absolutely nothing was learned. That which is learned, I contend, has to do with those beliefs and attitudes regarding linguistic diversity that are valued, or held to be an expression of truth, by certain members of this society in this time. Further, because the attitudes regarding language differences are inextricably intertwined with those regarding cultural differences, what is considered the "same" or "other" in terms of the values of Americans may well have its roots in the mediation taking place between cultures in the foreign language classroom.

It then becomes an issue of great significance when the foreign language class, through the processes I referred to as geographic fragmentation or English/American synonymy, for example, creates in the minds of the college-bound and college graduates of U.S. society a cultural referent of what constitutes *foreignness*. When this educational context then takes on the role of primarily a "filter" course with a social expectation of failure in regard to student proficiency, the very context that could strengthen democratic principles of equality in relation to linguistic and cultural differences finds itself operating to construct ideological frameworks diametrically opposed to its best potential. Beyond attitudes or conceptualizations of "American," *foreignness*, and the nature of language, though, the foreign language classroom contributes to a variety of sociocultural conflict phenomena described by critical theorists. The next chapter gives names to many elements of these cultural struggles through the language of critical pedagogy.

QUESTIONS FOR REFLECTION

How does the "failure" of language instruction in the United States reflect society's lack of interest in making its success a priority?

Who could benefit from a language education program "failing"?
How?

EXAMPLES TO CONSIDER

At this point we will begin to sharpen our skills in critical reflection by making some general observations about relationships of power demonstrated in the context and content of language education. This context and content dichotomy will become increasingly important as we continue to examine the foreign language classroom, because it is just such dichotomies that enable us to see the ideological and power relationships underlying curricula (Apple 1995; Jameson 1971; Williams 1977).

In the case of South Africa under the apartheid regime, for example, language education was typically divided into mother tongue and second language instruction. Though the mother tongue instructional rhetoric typically included empowering native speakers of languages, the educational context resulted in a de facto segregation of students into language, and thus socioeconomic, groups. Post-apartheid South Africa, however, with its 11 official languages, finds that English continues to gain in status because its value as a lingua franca enables those language education programs to capitalize on what Pennycook (1995) refers to as "English in the world" and "the world in English"—the global status afforded the language. In other words, it is the context in which language education programs in South Africa and elsewhere operate that create and sustain unequal power relationships (Reagan 1986). Those relationships are reflected, resisted, and reproduced within the language educational context.

Not only the context of language education but also the content of a course can reflect elements of cultural, political, and economic struggle. In the 1980s, before the fall of the Berlin Wall in 1989, East German foreign language courses in English used a textbook in which the sociocultural and political content of the selections are evident to U.S. readers of today. Given that the German Democratic Republic was considered part of the Soviet bloc, it was customary that educational contexts would undermine any citizen's confidence in the promises of U.S.-American democracy. Consider the following language textbook excerpt in relation to that set of goals:

A conversation sprang up, dealing first of all with what they had
seen on their tour [of the Cape Cod peninsula].

Marcus: You wanted us to see Cape Cod, the place where the "Mayflower" landed, Eileen! This is a very lovely place, it really is!

José: That's just how I feel! And I can understand that a student of history is interested in such places.

Eileen: It means more for me. The humanist ideas of the "Mayflower Compact" and the Declaration of Independence are part of our national heritage. I am sometimes a little bit worried at the thought of what has become of the old democratic ideals of America as the "land of hope for mankind."

José: That's right. I can only agree with what you just said. The ruling class has betrayed these ideals and the fight for them still goes on. (Böse, Lademann, and Schneider 1989, 45)

Furthermore, in their text, Böse, Lademann, and Schneider (1989) were able to incorporate ideological elements into the discussion of theoretically neutral grammatical material: related participles. An example of the *concessive* read "Though writing under capitalist conditions, he committed himself to the cause of socialism" (107).

QUESTIONS FOR DISCUSSION

Which careers require fluency in non-English languages in the United States? Compare and contrast educational backgrounds, relative pay and status, and proficiency required in the examples you cite.

How should teachers of language feel about issues of equity in terms of language status? Are language classrooms simply reflections of social struggles or participants in the struggles? Could they be both?

Why have teacher preparation programs failed to address the issues raised by critical reflection to their students? How and why should this practice be changed?

NOTES

1. Appropriate terminology is indeed a difficult choice in relation to this educational domain. I have chosen the term *world language educator* to describe those who teach languages to non-native speakers in the United States, but I will use "foreign language" when the term or educational program itself is at issue.

2. Again, terminology is an issue. *American* should not be considered synonymous with *U.S.-American*, but it often is used as such in the United States and abroad. When I place the term *American* in quotation marks, I mean *U.S.-American*.

3. The quotes from language teachers and students that follow were given, under condition of anonymity, during a pilot ethnographic study of a secondary foreign language department in East Hartford, Connecticut. The study was conducted during the fall of 1997.

4. For a more detailed discussion of the elements of power in a foreign language classroom, see Reagan and Osborn (1998).

Chapter 3

The Language
of Critical Pedagogy

The language of critical pedagogy, like other languages, does not always describe things that are foreign to us; it simply expresses those
things with more or less precision, and provides referents from which
positive academic and social discourse can proceed. In this chapter, I
will strike the balance between the intricate and sometimes contradictory complexities of critical educational theory and the need of accessibility for pre-service and in-service teachers who may be unfamiliar
with the field. The insights of critical theory are not reducible to a single
chapter in this or any text, and this section is not intended to serve as an
introduction to critical pedagogy.[1] Instead, we will look at how typical
elements of education can be understood utilizing the awareness afforded through reflection in terms of sociocultural power relationships.

Let us consider the hypothetical stories of four students: Allen, Brendon, Charles, and David. They are four males who were schooled in the
United States. Allen comes from a home in which the cultural values
and ideas are similar to those of the dominant class. Brendon, Charles,
and David are from homes in which the cultural backgrounds or values
differ in some significant way, including perhaps language, from the
dominant class.

Allen and Brendon graduated from high school, went on to college, and have been moderately successful in their careers. They are held up to students in the schools from which they graduated as examples of what good can happen if you apply yourself. Both live in an affluent neighborhood. Both are on track to upper-level management.

Charles, on the other hand, did not graduate from high school. He complained that school was "boring" at many times, and he often did not understand why he had to take certain classes. Despite an intelligence level similar to Allen and Brendon, his grades were abysmal. His scores on standardized tests in his early academic career were similar to those of Brendon and David. He eventually dropped out, commenting to his friends, "I just can't handle that school stuff."

David graduated high school and attended the local community college. He completed his associate's degree and went to work in a local business as a bookkeeper. He considered attending further college, but felt that the cost was prohibitive. His employer has offered to reimburse some of his tuition if he chooses to pursue the degree, since David's talent is obvious, and he would likely be an excellent office manager. From his perspective, however, David cannot see how he can afford to do so with a growing family.

The stories of these fictitious students are not unlike those of many in the United States. Many students whose cultural backgrounds resemble those of the dominant class, and fewer students whose backgrounds are different graduate high school and go to college. But many others fail to continue to the levels of education that equate with their potential.

QUESTIONS FOR REFLECTION

Think of students you have taught or have known. How do their stories resemble those of the fictitious students above? How do they differ?

How does educational success translate to success in one's career? What kinds of exceptions to a general rule can you name?

EXPLAINING EDUCATIONAL SUCCESSES AND FAILURES

The stories of Allen, Brendon, Charles, and David can be understood from a variety of perspectives, though in educational thought in the United States we typically see three paradigms from which the interpretations proceed. The first is known generally as positivism, and like the others makes some assumptions about the nature of truth and the purpose of education.

To the positivist, metaphorically, truth is a constant. Out there, somewhere, truth exists and if we can understand enough smaller pieces of it we can begin to perceive the overall picture of truth. Positivism makes sense when one is referring to the natural world. There are certain rules of physics and aerodynamics that, as we have grown in our understanding of them, have enabled humans to build flying machines that empower us to do what for most of our history was only for the birds. Understanding the principles of lift and drag as they relate to modern flight is possible partly because of carefully controlled investigations into the component parts of the phenomenon.

Positivism does not translate well to education, especially since its proponents tend to rely on quantifying phenomena to explain and predict events. When dealing with humans, there is not likely one best way to teach, since individuals teach other individuals, the permutations of personality mixes and behaviors become infinite. Positivistic approaches to education remain popular, however, because of their usefulness in setting policy. Comparing funding formulas with scores on standardized tests provides useful analysis and appealing argumentation for some, despite the fact that the assumptions underlying the logic are lacking.

The interpretivist typically rejects the positivistic interpretation of educational events. To the interpretivist, truth should be considered as a variable and is based on the perceptions and background of the person encountering the phenomena. In dealing with teaching, interpretivism is useful because it encourages teachers to individualize instruction such that each student constructs his or her own meaning and makes personal connections with the course material. As a result, learning becomes more meaningful and student motivation is enhanced.

Interpretivists, often aligning themselves with the processes of qualitative research (i.e., qualifying rather than quantifying phenomena), are extremely commonplace in contemporary United States education. Lessons are structured to draw as many connections as possible to the students' worlds. However, in terms of educational administration, data generated in such a fashion are considered "messy" or "fuzzy," and proceeding from them to policymaking becomes a challenging task.

Both of these paradigms, positivism and interpretivism, however, share an assumption about the four students in our story. They argue that the schooling process worked for Allen and Brendon, and to a lesser extent David, but failed for Charles. Thus the researchers and policymakers who ascribe to either paradigm set about trying to fix the educational process. The positivists would attempt to discover the natural laws underlying teaching and learning and applying them appropriately. The interpretivists would attempt to understand why Charles could not find personal meaning in his coursework. David's case would likely be problematic for either group of theorists, partly because of their failure to take into account the sociopolitical realities that interact with cultural backgrounds, values, and so on, and how these interactions affect educational outcomes. It is this aspect of understanding which benefits from critical analysis and reflection.

To the critical theorist, truth is better understood with the metaphor of being exponential, that is, raised by some power. In other words, truth in the form of explaining educational success and failure, and truth presented in the classroom as knowledge, is rooted in a set of power relationships. By rejecting the neutrality of truth and knowledge as presented in United States education, the practitioner can move toward a more effective and equitable practice. Let us begin the process by reviewing the story of Allen, Brendon, Charles, and David from a critical perspective.

CULTURE AS COMMODITY, REVISITED

Perhaps the most fundamental way in which to set apart critical educational theorists from their positivist and interpretivist counterparts is to focus on a single question: "Is education working for all students?" The positivists and interpretivists would point to overall successes but would indicate ways in which we could make education work better. Critical theorists, though by no means completely united in thought on the issues, generally agree that schooling is working to create or continue social inequity. In other words, though certain students fail, the educational systems we have are working; they are doing so to ends, however, that violate the principles of democratic education. By focusing both on the learning environment (i.e., the classroom) and the environment of learning (i.e., the social, cultural, political, and historical contexts of schooling), critical theorists break rank with other educational theorists to tackle fundamental questions related to how the theories and concepts that shape educational practice include inherent power relationships. Many go on to suggest that, by making oppressed members of society aware of their own situations, liberation from the oppressive forces can result (Biesta 1998).

In describing the four students in the illustration, I pointed out that the differences between the four were primarily related to cultural background and values. In critical terms, they entered school with different "ways of talking, acting, and socializing, as well as language practices, values, and styles of dress and behavior" (McLaren 1998, 193). This *cultural capital* reflects connections to a broader social identity that can be defined based on race, class, ethnicity, status, or any other of a myriad of constructions. It is important to note, however, that there are not naturally superior or preferred varieties of cultural capital, but that through the mediation process in the schools (and elsewhere) the capital of the dominant group appears to take on such qualities. The concept, for example, that one way of knowing is superior, is one that is formed, reformed, and resisted in the schools.

As an example, let us consider the following competing points of view regarding health and sickness: traditional medicine or alternative medicine. Within the terminology itself one can detect bias, but it is perhaps best to speak of how these two fields suggest that something counts as evidence. Certainly advances in understanding the human body have led to an eradication of many diseases. Though doctors will admit they often do not know exactly how a person recovers from an illness, they know that based on scientific research the human organism responds in predictable ways to various pharmaceutical interventions. Other medical professionals firmly believe that a body contains much of its own healing power, and that holistic approaches to treatment that focus on enabling the human body to achieve forms of balance are best to maintain health and cure disease. Proponents of traditional medicine tend to point to clinical studies with confidence as proof, whereas alternative medicine practitioners and patients allow for anecdotal evidence, such as stories from patients and knowledge gleaned from nonclinical sources (indeed even knowledge rooted in cultural lore) to be used as evidence of potential efficacy.

In the school systems of America these ways of knowing are not considered as equally valid alternatives. Proponents of both traditional and alternative medicine have until recently largely dismissed the claims of dissimilar professionals, at times even pointing with some ridicule at the opposing stance. The schools, however, over time inculcate in students a sense of expectation of scientific proof for those matters that are less controversial, often with the introduction and reinforcement of the scientific method.

My point here is not to argue traditional versus alternative medicine. I want instead to draw attention to the fact that this balance of argument as expressed in the schools of the United States, though perhaps differing in regions of the country, is actually based on a sociopolitical and historical framework. It is doubtful that years ago any medical theory cast in contradiction to empirical principles would have seen such resistance in the educational system (for example, the practice of trephining, drilling circular holes in the skulls of mentally ill patients to release demonic spirits, is certainly beyond the current empiricist paradigm). Similarly, if in the future certain groups in the United States were in power politically, there is no doubt that the balance could, and likely would, shift again.

Yet the "facts" as expressed by proponents of both theoretical stances would not have changed. Truth in this instance is not a constant nor a variable, because neither group could be said to disprove the other, and it is equally doubtful that some people are cured only by traditional medicine whereas others are cured only by alternative medicine, based on differing perspectives. Instead, the cultural capital (in terms of how a group of people "know" something) of segments of society is systematically devalued, either completely or partially, by the educational system.

But such dramatic cases are not the only points on which cultural capital as expressed by different groups is mediated by the educational system. The schools regularly devalue the cultural capital of those groups in instances where such capital varies from that of the dominant culture. Eye contact with the teacher is important in most classrooms for students who are to be academically successful. The music of Mozart and Beethoven is valued above that of rap and country by the institutions of education in the United States. And that form of English mistakenly described as "standard" is considered much more valuable than ebonics or Southern dialect, and more appropriate for this society than any non-English language.

Those students whose cultural capital is devalued by the educational system find themselves marginalized in the society as a whole. By *marginalization*, I refer to the way in which certain voices in society (usually identified by social grouping) tend to be placed on the fringes of the political power spectrum. As racial and gender inequalities in the corridors of power have demonstrated, the country where "all men are created equal" is still governed primarily by men, mostly white men. These men all view the world in much the same way (regardless of political party, one should add), though their views of the role of government might differ. They have been educated in such a way that their mental frameworks, their organization of knowledge and truth, and the ways in which they make sense of the world are comparable. This ideological similarity often prevents them from understanding the plight of the less powerful and oppressed. They point out those who remain marginalized to students of diversity in color or gender or class, for instance, who have "made it" as models of how to be successful. By and large their intentions may be sincere. It is their understanding of social reality that is short-sighted.

The schools fail to declare to their students the subjectivity and social, political, economic, and historical context that they teach as truth. The graduates are not taught to think in these terms because the schools' function extends beyond (or, better said, not up to) the point of human enlightenment. Schools also serve to prepare the next generation of members of society to function in that society. The plethora of ways beyond formal course content in which they do so, referred to as a *hidden curriculum*, however, tends to favor the reproduction of existing social orders. The hidden curriculum is that program of socialization in the schools that runs parallel to the explicit curriculum and inherently serves to benefit those whose cultural capital resembles that of the dominant culture, thus marginalizing others. It is the hidden curriculum that explains the preponderance of male success in math and science, the dearth of funding for the arts, and the failure of foreign language education to produce competent bilinguals in the United States. This social curriculum is not as hidden as the name implies. Expectations regarding behavior in schools in the United States are quite explicit in many instances. It is the power relationships underlying this school program that are primarily hidden.

Using this basic form of understanding the roles of schools in reproducing the status quo, one can begin to perceive the power relationships underlying the educational success and failure stories of our four students. However, the explanation of schooling from a critical perspective to this point has been intentionally reduced and grossly oversimplified. As a result, though we can well explain Allen and David, Brendon and Charles are still problematic to understand.

Allen, the member of the dominant culture, was able to successfully navigate the educational mediation because he identified with, indeed was a product of, that dominant cultural transmission. David, though, could identify his "limitations" that were socially imposed. As a result, he was relegated both systemically and by his own ideological perceptions to a certain career pinnacle.

Brendon, though, is a member of a traditionally marginalized group yet seems to have been able to overcome and be successful. Charles, on the other hand, dropped out. Certainly one should not argue that schools would encourage that behavior in the case of a student with such potential.

There have been several critical studies and writings that have helped us to understand the role of resistance in the reproduction of sociocultural power relationships. Willis (1977), in his influential ethnography *Learning to Labour*, described the resistance of working-class boys to the educational system in England. McRobbie (1978), as well, noted that young females rejected the roles prescribed for them related to marriage and sexuality. Common to these and other studies about resistance to educational mediation of culture is that the resistance itself resulted in the marginalization of the individuals (see Shor 1986). As Apple (1995) clarifies, the rejection of the hidden curriculum carried with it a rejection of the explicit curriculum and a subsequent reproduction of social order. The phenomenon occurred, in part, because the rejection of educational mediation results in exclusion from the societal benefits of being educated.

The complicity of the educational system in the case of our fictitious Charles is perhaps obvious. Charles rejected the cultural mediation, the "school stuff," but in doing so participated in his own marginalization. However, the progressivist and constructivist solutions to the problem of making the curriculum more relevant to students like Charles are deceptively oversimplified. In essence, it could be argued that Charles recognized the inequity of the system and made a rational decision not to contribute to the charade. As a result, the educational system may have been quite relevant to his life in that it demonstrated the message in regard to his cultural capital, a message that was also heard by Brendon.

Brendon succeeded because he was able to assimilate or acculturate to the dominant culture and to adopt many of its mental frameworks and other ideological elements. Brendon is a success story not because he overcame odds or applied himself; indubitably he did both. Brendon was successful to the extent that he was able to become a part of the dominant culture. I stress *to the extent* because if Brendon differs in ways that he cannot change, such as race, he will still find significant obstacles in a system fashioned to protect and promote the dominant culture. And if Brendon were *Brenda*, a female, then her obstacles, such as the one referred to as the "glass ceiling," would be even more pronounced.

Though the cases of Brendon and Charles demonstrate how the dominant culture can incorporate those who understand, at some level, the inner workings of the system, it is the fact that all of the characters in this story consent to the role of dominator or dominated that creates what is referred to as *hegemony*. Hegemony, simply put, is the process of consensual dominance of the subordinate culture by the dominant culture. Both parties consent to the arrangement. But why?

It is important to note that in some instances the consent is obtained because the mechanisms of control are not seen, because they are disguised in "neutral" and commonsense assumptions or because the promise of success to those who would consent is personally appealing. It is in the case of the former, or the disguising of relationships, that the foreign language classroom plays its most active role. By creating cultural referents of what is *foreignness*, voices can be marginalized that differ from those of the dominant culture. And the college-bound students of the United States are not even aware that such ideological frameworks, while seeming to be commonsense, are at least in part traceable to the educational context of the foreign language classroom. It is the ability to disguise the relationship as a label that is quite serious in terms of social justice. The curriculum, both in explicit and hidden forms, is complicit in the process.

Language curricula unavoidably embody dominant cultural values that become elements of hegemony by perpetuating the normative "buy-in" of educated, dominant language speakers. "Educated" members of a society believe that what they learned in foreign language classes, for example, was neutral, apolitical knowledge, when in actuality the curriculum served the interests of the dominant language group. This dominance is achieved by hindering the access to power of linguistic minorities through the creation of a commonsense assumption that non-English languages in the United States are a form of *foreignness*, while leaving in place an ideological tension between promoting foreign language education and subsequently devaluing bilingualism. It is the case that the failure of foreign language instruction represents success in terms of hegemony.

Though the ideologies that underlie foreign language education may be more difficult to ascertain due to the specialized nature of the field, it is important to note that there is not necessarily a shared ideology between agents in foreign language education, including, but not limited to, teachers and the state. In other words, the field may well include opposing positions as teachers strive to translate to students a love for language diversity and learning.

QUESTIONS FOR REFLECTION

Language education in the United States can be divided into foreign language and ESL/bilingual education. How might the language of critical pedagogy explain this division?

Can education be "fixed" to the point of being neutral? Why or why not? If not, what should educators in a democracy seek to provide students?

STANDARDS AND *FOREIGNNESS*

Johnson (1991), reiterated by Apple (1996) in *Cultural Politics and Education*, makes an argument worth considering as we begin our discussion of standards:

> A common curriculum, in a heterogeneous society, is not a recipe for "cohesion," but for resistance and the renewal of divisions. Since it always rests on cultural foundations of its own, it will put pupils in their places, not according to "ability," but according to how their cultural communities rank along the criteria taken as "standard." (79)

Our discussion here is intended to begin to highlight some of those assumptions in the field of foreign language education. We will confine ourselves at this point to the *Standards for Foreign Language Learning: Preparing for the 21st Century* (1996). Though often referred to as the "ACTFL standards" or the "Five C's" (Communication, Cultures, Connections, Comparisons, and Communities), the standards actually represent a collaborative effort of ACTFL, the American Association of

Teachers of French (AATF), the American Association of Teachers of German (AATG), and the American Association of Teachers of Spanish and Portuguese (AATSP). This document represents for foreign language education a significant achievement as the field attempts to take its place among "core" subject areas like math and social studies.

It is also germane to understand what the *Standards* are meant to be; as an excerpt from the document explains,

> The standards do not describe the current status of foreign language education in this country. While they reflect the best instructional practice, they do not describe what is being attained by the majority of foreign language students. *The Standards for Foreign Language Learning* will not be achieved overnight; rather they provide a gauge against which to measure improvement in the years to come. (National Standards in Foreign Language Education Project 1996, 25)

The standards, though not claiming to depict practice as it exists, are written to practitioners and planners who are currently in practice as a regulative ideal. The authors themselves acknowledge this fact in two places: "Standards have defined the agenda for the next decade—and beyond" (National Standards in Foreign Language Education Project 1996, 15) and in the acknowledgments as the authors thank "the collaborating organizations and the Board of Directors for demonstrating the power that professional unity can achieve" (5). Solomon (1997) reported on preliminary results of a national survey on changes in local curricula due to the introduction of the *Standards*. Almost half of the schools responded that their curriculum had changed due to an awareness of the standards. The *Standards* provide information regarding the direction in which foreign language educators as a collective entity hope to move, but even more, provide insight into the assumptions currently made and the intellectual-ideological frameworks in place in the field.

In the introduction to the *Standards* one finds, for example, a statement that reveals a presumably shared connection between producer and interpreter (i.e., the authors and the readers) of the text:

> From the flowing green lawns and porch swings of rural America to the front stoops of our cities, ours has traditionally been a culture of openness, of passing the time of day with friends who stroll

by—coming to our doors to question and discuss, to request our aid, to bring rich gifts. And since the street leads in both directions, we are going out into the wide world to run *our* errands. (National Standards in Foreign Language Education Project 1996, 11)

Flowing green lawns and porch swings may certainly remind one of Norman Rockwell's America, but the description idealizes both urban and rural intercultural relations. The issue becomes clear when one thinks of the city, the stoops, and the neighbors who stroll by in comparison with another description, this time provided by Jonathan Kozol (1991) in *Savage Inequalities*:

Taxi drivers refused to take me to some of these schools and would deposit me a dozen blocks away, in border areas beyond which they refused to go. I'd walk the last half-mile on my own. Once, in the Bronx, a woman stopped her car, told me I should not be walking there, insisted I get in, and drove me to the school. I was dismayed to walk or ride for blocks and blocks through neighborhoods where every face was black, where there were simply *no white people anywhere*. (5)

The idealized neighborhoods described in the *Standards* do not exist in the United States, but the depiction of an "us" who encounter a "them" continues to be a common theme.

The document includes a list of reasons, quoted above, why all of these "neighbors" were coming in contact with one another: "to question and discuss, to request our aid, to bring rich gifts. And since the street leads in both directions, we are going out into the wide world to run *our* errands." Elsewhere in the *Standards,* the reader is informed as to why people who are communicatively competent in foreign languages use the languages: "They converse, argue, criticize, request, convince, and explain effectively" (National Standards in Foreign Language Education Project 1996, 36). Except for "converse," the other terms in these lists seem to indicate either distance or conflict (question and discuss, argue, criticize, convince, and explain effectively) or economic loss or gain (request aid, bring rich gifts, run errands).

The connection of foreign language education to economic gain is a common one. Yet the ideological frameworks we are exploring here are likely not the result of intentional planning by the writers of the document. Instead, I would argue, as professionals in the field of foreign language education, these individuals have also been introduced, inculcated, or perhaps indoctrinated into the mental frameworks (i.e., *foreignness*) underlying the assumptions.

The introduction to the *Standards* also contains many affirmations of the educational value of foreign language learning. Further, there seem to be attempts to argue that foreign language classrooms are "equal playing fields," no doubt to counteract a long-standing belief that foreign language education is only for the educated elite: "[I]t was shown that the economic background of foreign language students did not affect performance; students from lower socioeconomic levels who studied foreign languages performed on a par with their more affluent peers" (National Standards in Foreign Language Education Project 1996, 12). Through claiming that successful foreign language study is meritocratic, the implementation of standards can be justified as benchmark measures of objective success, and foreign language skill can be measured in terms of degrees. Since many students on the lower socioeconomic levels already speak two languages, it is doubtful that such a claim could be true, given the generally recognized benefits of bilingualism on learning yet another language. In essence, if all of the commonly held assumptions were true, bilingual students on lower socioeconomic levels should perform *better* in foreign language classrooms.

In a variety of other places, the *Standards* reinforce the value of language study for economic reasons (including mention of the labor market), and leisure activities, including tourism. The authors have also reiterated the traditional reasons for the importance of studying foreign languages, with the exception of its relationship to "high culture" or a recognized historical relationship to Western educational tradition. They have, however, stressed the role that foreign language education may play in helping students understand cultural differences, at the same time failing to escape the assumptions associated with the idea of something "unusual" to find foreign languages in place in the United States. To examine this issue, though, it is important to begin with the way the text itself addresses the issue of *foreignness*:

> The use of the word "foreign" to describe the teaching of languages other than English is becoming increasingly problematic within the U.S. context. Many of the languages taught within our schools are not "foreign" to many of our students (e.g., Italian, Chinese, or Spanish), nor are they "foreign" to the United States

(e.g., Native American languages, American Sign Language, Spanish, or French). Many states have recognized this situation by referring to these languages as World Languages, Modern and Classical Languages, Languages Other Than English (LOTEs), or Second Languages, to name a few of the terms used. The members of the standards task force debated this issue many times over the three year project period. *In the end, the term "foreign language" was maintained in the title of the document because it is readily understood by all prospective audiences.* Within the document, however, the decision was made to avoid the term "foreign" whenever possible. Hence, the terms *"second language," "target language," and sometimes simply "language" are all used interchangeably to refer to languages other than English taught as an academic subject.* (National Standards in Foreign Language Education Project 1996, 23, italics added)

An acknowledgment that the term "foreign" fits most appropriately into the reference frame for both producer and interpreter of the text draws attention to this "otherness" at the same time that the document distinguishes between English as a second language (ESL) instruction and foreign language instruction.

This distinction between ESL and foreign languages represents a conflict embedded within the *Standards*, many curricula and textbooks, and the profession itself. All of the praise of foreign language learning seems to be applied either to native English speakers learning "foreign" languages or speakers of a nondominant language learning another "foreign" language. The *Standards* fall short of equating foreign language teaching with ESL instruction, a distinction that is sociological, not pedagogical.

Though the authors are careful at the beginning to explain that native speakers and non-native speakers of English should both learn foreign languages, the assumptions made within do not apply to both sets of prospective students, and again tend to discount the already existing linguistic diversity within the United States. In describing the applications of the benchmarks of progress, for example, a reader finds

the cultural differences embedded in the study of non-European languages may be more readily apparent than the cultural differences in European languages. Similar challenges exist when working with visual languages (e.g., American Sign Language), languages which are no longer spoken (e.g., Latin and Ancient Greek), and languages with no written component (e.g., some Native American languages). (National Standards in Foreign Language Education Project 1996, 25)

This claim is repeated within the *Standards* in varying forms (see, for example, 34), but it actually reveals an assumption that language learners will be more familiar with European languages than non-European ones. If, for example, I am a native speaker of Chinese, then learning another Asian language may well be easier than learning a European language.

Related to this issue is what the *Standards* authors describe as an American mindset (32). The *Standards* claim that interpreting text means the ability to understand or comprehend a foreign language text based on an informed cultural understanding, which is then contrasted as being more than comprehension with an "American mindset." The assumption inherent here, perhaps reflecting the view of many, is that Americans are monocultural. Though it reminds one of the joke about speakers of two languages being bilingual, three trilingual, and one an American, this description of monoculturalism adds another nationalistic element to language proficiency. The implication is that it is outside of the mainstream experience, even "un-American," to be bicultural.

Another, more disturbing, element in the *Standards* relates to heritage language (non-native speakers of English learning their own language as "foreign") learners:

> Similar modifications will need to be made when applying the standards to students who have a home background in the language studied. As stated previously, these students may come to class able to converse in the language in home and community situations, but may lack the ability to interact comfortably in more formal settings. (National Standards in Foreign Language Education Project 1996, 25)

The tacit assumption here is that heritage language learners do not possess the linguistic skills necessary for high social prestige language use. This assumption reflects a stereotype of Americans who speak languages other than English.

The *Standards* also include some discussion of the benefits a heritage language learner can reap when discovering how varieties of their language reflect cultural differences. As an example, the authors cite the varieties of Spanish used throughout the world. However, in no instance is there a discussion of British English, Australian English, Southern dialect, or any other form of English being considered appropriate for "foreign" language study. The omission reflects the bias that only English cannot be foreign within this context.

Finally, the *Standards* attempt to extol the virtues of multilingual communities:

> Some students are fortunate to have direct access to multilingual communities through their home backgrounds; all students benefit from an awareness of the many communities in the U.S. where English and other languages are spoken—communities such as the French-speaking Cajun areas of Louisiana, the German areas of the Texas Hill Country, the Italian communities of the Northeast, the Spanish-speaking communities of the Southwest, and the Asian neighborhoods of the West Coast. (National Standards in Foreign Language Education Project 1996, 49–50)

The effect of this passage is to localize or regionalize linguistic diversity. It is not, according to the implication here, a national phenomenon in every neighborhood. It is limited to single languages in certain geographic areas. Certainly the intent here was to show that linguistic diversity is widespread; however, it allows for *foreignness* to take on geographic boundaries by failing to acknowledge that in every neighborhood the linguistically diverse are "strolling by."

The discussion presented in this chapter is not intended to serve as a condemnation of the *Standards*. That document, due to its significance in the contemporary and future practice of foreign language education in the United States, is best suited for an examination of the conceptualizations in our field. The *Standards* contain elements reflecting the beliefs of many educators regarding the relative status enjoyed by languages in the United States. But the differences as depicted within this document, textbooks, other curricula, and even classroom practice in the United States contribute to a conceptualization of *foreignness*, despite the claims by curricularists that cultural comparisons should lead to greater understanding. Instead, the approaches currently employed in terms of foreign language education in the schools contribute to another framework, discussed by critical theorists as *whiteness*.

Whiteness, it is important to point out, does not necessarily equate with skin color alone. Whiteness, as Peter McLaren (1998) explains,

> constitutes and demarcates ideas, feelings, knowledges, social practices, cultural formations, and systems of intelligibility that are identified with or attributed to white people and which are invested in by white people as "white" . . . . It both fixes and sustains discursive regimes that represent self and "other"; that is, whiteness represents a regime of differences that produces and racializes an abject other. . . . Whiteness displaces blackness and brownness—specific forms of non-whiteness—into signifiers of deviance and criminality within social, cultural, cognitive, and political contexts. (282–283)

In other words, whiteness is a set of frameworks of thought, unified in their focus on that which is deviant from itself. That focus may be in terms of defining, labeling, explaining or otherwise entering into discourse with the result of shaping social, cultural, cognitive, educational, historical, political, or economic practice or thought in such a way that it benefits those who control the discursive parameters. In the foreign language classroom, whiteness is that which supports the conceptualization of *foreignness*. It is the *this* defining the *that*, the *us* describing the *them*, and the *American* naming the *foreign*.

The goal of critical reflection in the foreign language classroom, then, is to use the language of critical pedagogy to challenge this process. Given the preponderance of those who benefit from whiteness within the foreign language classroom, critical reflection becomes a vehicle to examine what Henry Giroux refers to as the politics of multiculturalism. As Giroux (1997b) advocates:

> I want to argue that educators need to rethink the politics of multiculturalism as part of a broader attempt to engage the world of public and global politics. This suggests challenging the narratives of national identity, culture, and ethnicity as part of a pedagogical effort to provide dominant groups with the knowledge and histories to examine, acknowledge, and unlearn their own privilege. (236)

Critical reflection in the foreign language classroom will allow teachers to guide students into a consideration of cultural difference, without reducing those differences to measurable behavioral objectives or cultural blurbs at the end (or beginning) of textbook chapters. Teachers can challenge the narratives of *foreignness* and encourage their students to do the same.

CONCLUSION

This chapter was intended to introduce foreign language teachers to the language of critical pedagogy as it can be applied within our own field. There are, naturally, significant pieces that have been generalized and a continuing need for exhaustive analysis of this educational context. One goal of this text is to open the door to that analysis in classrooms across the country daily.

In this way, the foreign language classroom provides a unique educational context in which the real world applications of critical pedagogy can be realized. The incorporation of theory into practice in this way can revitalize language instruction beyond rearranging grammatical syllabi or simply adding a veneer of cultural, communicative, or contextual activities. If teacher educators and teachers alike will fundamentally reexamine the nature of language education in the United States in terms of power, the nexus between critical reflection and emancipatory praxis in our context can become clear. Redefining the parameters from which academic and social dialogue proceed, "foreign" language teachers will seize back the classrooms from those who would strip their pedagogical talents to make them merely managers of classroom behavior. The language of critical pedagogy will assist, even empower, teachers who want to argue that their role is greater than simply preparing the next labor force. And critical reflection will require courage—courage to take small steps toward a larger goal, the redefinition of language education in the United States.

QUESTIONS FOR DISCUSSION

How could the language of critical pedagogy be used to challenge the content of language courses?

Could language courses be expanded or changed to address issues raised by critical pedagogues? How?

How are standards and prescribed curricula able to contribute to cultural mediation in the classroom?

If your students became aware of the issues raised in this text so far, how might you advise them to act on their newfound knowledge?

NOTE

1. Several texts do provide such an introduction, notably the third edition of Peter McLaren's *Life in Schools* (1998, Longman), Joan Wink's *Critical Pedagogy: Notes from the Real World* (1997, Longman), and the second edition of *Critical Pedagogy: An Introduction* (1999, Greenwood Press) by Barry Kanpol.

Chapter 4

How to Reflect, Critically

Defining reflective practice is becoming more difficult as the term has grown to mean something different to almost everyone who uses it (see Brookfield 1995; Smyth 1992; Zeichner 1994). When one then speaks of *critical* reflection, definitions are even more difficult to find. Brookfield (1995), though, provides a description that is useful for framing our discussion of critical reflection in foreign language classrooms:

> [C]ritical reflection is inherently ideological. It is also morally grounded. It springs from a concern to create the conditions under which people can learn to love one another, and it alerts them to the forces that prevent this. Being anchored in values of justice, fairness, and compassion, critical reflection finds its political representation in the democratic process . . . [encouraging] us to create conditions under which each person is respected, valued, and heard. (26–27)

As another point of departure for understanding critical reflection in the foreign language classroom, let us examine one claim of Brubacher, Case, and Reagan (1994) in their text on building a culture of inquiry in the schools:

In developing transformational curricula, it is essential that teachers go beyond traditional teaching methods and materials. Textbooks, for instance, should at best be seen as points of departure
for the curriculum rather than as curricular guides themselves.
The distinction between curriculum and instruction is at best misleading; there is a symbiotic relationship between them that the
teacher must take into account. (74)

Their statement leads us to understand that the commonly accepted
categories of curriculum and instruction are not mutually exclusive do-
mains, but that within these commonly accepted mental frameworks,
there exist elements of symbiosis, of negotiation, of dialectic. It is
within and beyond that space that critical reflection works to define, to
test, and to trace underlying power structures.

Critical reflection involves challenging the boundaries of our educational thought and practice and rearranging or dissecting the constructs that we employ in an effort to understand the relations of
power that underlie them. It is ideological and moral, yes, but it is
also disquieting. Critical reflection should not result in lengthy,
complex lists of the essential or base elements of equitable praxis in
the foreign language classroom, but ideally should lead us to discover that the parameters of our theory and practice, our curriculum
and instruction, our language and culture are inherently *context dependent*. The aspects of this context include social, cultural, political,
economic, historical, and other categories associated with the interaction of human beings within a society. Those who crave simple,
unchanging formulas within which to structure their teaching or
thought will not find critical reflection comforting. Those who recognize the social conditions placed on the production of knowledge
may find it empowering.

I will suggest a genesis for the foreign language teacher in regard to
a process of critical reflection. I stress that the framework is tentative
and intended only to provide a point from which critically reflective
skills should grow. It is not a magical formula guaranteed to improve
practice and the process itself should be engaged critically as well.

To engage in critical reflection in the classroom, teachers can consider the following:

1. Attempt to describe elements of theory or practice as they are found,
   at first without attribution of suspected power relationships involved.

2. Examine the role of the elements in terms of curriculum and instruction. Why is each element found within the classroom? Which broader educational objectives does it purport to advance?
3. Examine the role of the elements in terms of the societal context. Within the United States, what relevance might they have for specific cultural, ethnic, gender, racial, socioeconomic or other groups?
4. Given the starting thesis that the school mediates between different segments of society, how do your descriptions of the classroom and the societal context reflect that mediation? Could certain segments benefit from the educational results?
5. What could be changed so that the ideological underpinnings are effectively challenged? How might theory or practice be altered?

This structure allows for some flexibility while reflecting a content and context dichotomy common to critical analysis (see Apple 1995; Bernstein 1990; Jameson 1971; Lanigan, 1981; Lawton 1975; Williams 1977). A simpler form of the procedure above is as follows:

1. Detached description
2. Relevance for the classroom
3. Relevance in society
4. Relevance in cultural struggle
5. From practice to praxis

DETACHED DESCRIPTION

To begin, a description of the point or points of analysis, usually a theoretical construct, textbook presentation, or classroom practice, provides the teacher with an opportunity to segue from the role of active participant to participant observer. Journaling, for both the teacher and students, can provide a vivid form of case description from which they draw.

At this stage in the process, the teacher attempts to record as many of the events or elements of analysis before beginning to assign value to them. For example, "The student was distracted during the presentation of vocabulary," though not as value-laden as "The student behaved rebelliously," could be better expressed as "While the teacher reviewed vocabulary items on the chalkboard, one male student passed a note to a peer, leafed through a magazine, and drew on his desk." This latter form of expression will contain elements that may be relevant as one begins to reflect on the broader spectrum of issues.

In essence, at this stage of critical reflection, the teacher attempts to be "clinical" in her or his description of the event, point, or theory. This form of "engaged detachment" recognizes the necessity of reflecting on practice specifically in terms of power relationships, while at the same time moving toward emancipatory praxis. Emancipatory praxis results as the ideologies that shape and, to a certain degree, control our thought and academic life are scrutinized under the lens of critical reflection. This scrutiny can be best accomplished when the values inherent in data are minimized (though especially note that the values will not be entirely removed).

RELEVANCE FOR THE CLASSROOM

The second phase of critical reflection, an analysis of the classroom rationale for elements of practice, may seem commonsensical. Why do we ask students to solve word problems in math? Because mathematical problems in life are rarely found already in equation form. Such an analysis should not stop there, however. Note that several assumptions are being made here that should also be grist for analysis. Math classes include word problems because students are required to complete such items on statewide assessments, which in turn are developed by humans who attempt to quantify student skills in mathematics. The word problems are also deemed important because mathematics classes are in the process of preparing students to function in a world in which math skills, even if sometimes presenting themselves quite differently from an equation, are essential. The theories that drive mathematical instruction, like other forms of instruction, likewise assume that for education to be successful it must be relevant to the students' current and future world. Moreover, math and science skills are significant aspects of international competition, in terms of technological and other forms of advanced development.

In a journal, these points of consideration can be written in paragraph form, numbered as a short list, or otherwise documented. It is important that the classroom analysis be traced, as specifically as possible, back to assumptions about human learning, the subject area, and schooling that in turn guide our practice. The theoretical constructs that guide practice, not only the elements of practice themselves, are of great concern in critical reflection. They provide the blueprint from which teachers engaged in critical reflection begin to decode the world of academe in which they work. This form of literacy is absolutely essential for teachers engaged in progressive practice and is all too often lacking in one's professional education.

RELEVANCE IN SOCIETY

The critical reflection must then move beyond the classroom, even attempting to temporarily divorce itself from the classroom for analysis. We need to examine the role of the subject matter, the applicable theories and practices of the educational process, and the roles differing segments of societies take as these elements are interrelated. Rather than simply looking for cause-effect relationships, however, we are to focus on contributions to cultural struggle. This point cannot be understated. Simple reductionist formulas that claim that aspects of schooling result in societal relations being configured as they are (or the idea that input always equals output) should be rejected. Instead, critically reflective teachers should strive to understand the school as a mediator of value in terms of cultural capital. As well, the competing pressures from society on the actors within the school context—that is, teachers, administrators, students, parents, and others—need to be discussed.

In the case of mathematics education, one might consider the role of mathematics in engineering and scientific careers, the advances in technology that place the United States in global competition with other nations, and the value placed by society on these factors as a framework within which the mathematics classes operate. As a result, if males are encouraged to perform in mathematics, they will tend to take their places in society as assigned such individuals. Those who reject being groomed for such positions will be less likely to achieve in this manner, and it could be argued that females would find the ideologies guiding curriculum and instruction in this discipline tend to devalue their success within it.

RELEVANCE IN CULTURAL STRUGGLE

The cultural struggle element of critical reflection is undoubtedly one of the most difficult. Constant revision and diligent observation of the workings of the society in which we live are necessary. Challenging every assumption, particularly those that we use to organize our thinking about the world around us, is essential. Hypothetical examinations of shifts in these assumptions will likewise help. For example, if the ability to bear children became one of great societal prestige, though not currently included within the reward systems of schools, how might one expect to see curricula change? Further, what form would resistance take from males, currently empowered but biologically hindered from benefiting from such a hypothetical change in societal value? These hypothetical examinations become the origin of possibilities to improve practice.

Stated differently, assume that the values of the dominant culture were different than they are. Given the current reflection of practice in the classroom and the orders of society, how would educational systems reflect a change in dominant cultural values? When the Nazis controlled Germany, for example, curricular stress on physical preparedness became more important than preparation to live as a citizen of the broader world. These curricular shifts reflected a very real change in dominant cultural beliefs while the Fascists were in power.

After mentally rearranging perceived cultural priorities, the teacher should consider how the struggles actually in place are reflected within contemporary practice and theories. The critically reflective practitioner begins to find the common thread between the description, the classroom, and the society, as it relates to struggle in all three. Having entered into a level of understanding that begins to highlight the interrelationships of theory and practice in the classroom with the cultural struggles in the societal context in which they operate, educators subjectify the schooling process—we show how that which seems neutral is in fact subjective, as filtered through the interests of the dominant culture.

FROM PRACTICE TO PRAXIS

And finally, given that the teacher's analysis is correct, what changes in practice would serve to disrupt the hegemony as it currently exists? Praxis, or theory-informed practice, develops into emancipatory praxis as the teacher intervenes to challenge the ideology or question the consent. This extension of critical reflection is necessary as teachers discover their roles as cultural workers. Some teachers have expressed a lack of confidence in their ability to become political and cultural agents. Yet it is precisely this role that they now occupy, and thus they can become agents of positive change (Bassey 1996).

To challenge ideology, teachers engage in behaviors that point out the power basis underlying mental constructs accepted as neutral or

natural. One effective way to accomplish this is to test the reorganization of mental frameworks. To question consent, the practitioner likewise points out to others the underlying power relationships within and
among various elements. Beyond this step, the teacher encourages students to explore how consent is related to effective domination. This
critical challenge can be carried out in a number of ways, either directly
or indirectly. In Chapter Six, I will discuss in detail some ways the foreign language teacher can challenge ideology and question consent.

Now let us work through some examples together. It is relevant to
remember that it is the process, not a particular product, that is the goal
of this exercise. Critical reflection is not an exact science and there are
no absolutely correct interpretations. Instead, one should seek to find
answers that are consistent among subject matter, practice, theory, society, and an understanding of power as seen in each. The effectiveness
of such interpretations is limited to an ability to see the workings of particular sociohistorical-dependent constructs.

QUESTIONS FOR REFLECTION

Begin keeping a critical reflection journal. What elements within practice do you seem to focus on first?

How does the difficulty we have in completing the phases of the process
reflect our own initiation into the ideologies that guide education?

WHO WRITES HISTORY?

Detached description: A student in a history class questions how the
imperialism of the Axis powers in World War II differs from the concept
of manifest destiny as expressed by the settlers of the New World.

Relevance for the classroom: Manifest destiny, or a belief that God intended for European Americans to expand the colonies to the western
coast of North America, is an important concept with which students of
history should be familiar, since it in part motivated the expansion from
colonial territories. The imperialism of Axis powers is likewise important, in part because it demonstrates the threat perceived by the allies
that led to the conflict.

Relevance in society: Understanding the motivations behind a nation's actions is an important component of living in a global society.
Standardized exams often mention such terms as imperialism or mani-

fest destiny, and people who are educated are expected to be familiar with them.

Relevance in cultural struggle: There is a tendency to utilize terminology to hide power relationships. Though "strategic initiative" and "nuclear buildup" can refer to the same policy or set of actions, the connotative weight of each is different. Likewise, that which is destiny can be understood as inevitable, and thus any actions associated with the concept could be considered unavoidable. Imperialism, on the other hand, carries a commonsense connotation of aggression or oppression, at least in contemporary use.

From practice to praxis: To challenge the ideology in this example, a teacher could, after explaining the importance of knowing the terms for test purposes, suggest that "manifest imperialism" might also describe the beliefs of those involved in westward expansion. The teacher could then suggest how the terms themselves serve to defend actions that might be deemed objectionable. The teacher could challenge consent by having students explore other concepts that seem historically neutral, but are in themselves reflecting the interests of the dominant culture. Students can trace how their consent to the ideology behind the terms is encouraged through the use of tests and other educational practices reflecting the "banking model."

History or the presentation of history in textbooks has drawn much criticism and examination from critical pedagogues. Jean Anyon's (1979) study of history textbooks twenty years ago led to a conclusion that is worth remembering today:

> The school curriculum has contributed to the formation of attitudes that make it easier for powerful groups, those whose knowledge is legitimized by school studies, to manage and control society. Textbooks not only express the dominant groups' ideology, but also help to form attitudes in support of their local position. Indeed the importance of ideology to the power of dominant groups increases as the use of overt social coercion declines. . . . Inasmuch as social choices are likely to be made on the basis of the social knowledge and symbolic meanings that are available, what one knows about social groups and processes is central to one's decisions. The perceived legitimacy of certain ideas increases their acceptance and utilization. . . . If the views embedded in the information disseminated by these agencies [schools] predispose people to accept some values and not others,

support some groups' activities and not others, and exclude some choices as unacceptable, then they provide invisible intellectual, internalized, and perhaps unconscious boundaries to social choice. (382–383)

But so often in language classes, we fail to expand on history beyond simple formulaic discussions of historical events. The horrors of the Holocaust and Nazi atrocities, for example, provide ample opportunity for discussion of political and cultural struggle as well as the role of language planning within such struggles. However, textbooks of French and German rarely include even a brief blurb. The skills of critical reflection are necessary in presentation of concepts in history, but even more so as one examines the cultural struggles implicit in the selection of great works of literature.

WHO WRITES LITERATURE?

Detached description: A teacher of language arts commonly requires students to journal as part of their writing development. One student, who describes herself as a Latina, points out that when the class studies literature translated from Spanish, it is always presented from overseas sources, not from those "in my own neighborhood." The teacher at first is surprised by the criticism, because it was her intention to have the students appreciate the cultural heritage of each other as presented in the literary selections.

Relevance for the classroom: The purpose the teacher had for incorporating literature from the Spanish language was to celebrate the diverse voices that could be found within the community. The assumptions relate to an attempt to make the classroom more democratic, which in turn must be done by letting students hear the Latin voices that are a part of their community. The teacher chose literature from Mexico and Spain that had been translated. The assumption here is that literature from those areas would be significantly different from the English language canon.

Relevance in society: At this point in this scenario, I will stop providing analysis and will ask some questions that you could use to frame your own responses. When we speak of diverse voices within the community, is it accurate to assume that literature written in the language spoken by those members is automatically representative of their voices? If you have as a student a child who has spent most of her life in the United States, would you expect Spanish or Mexican literature to be more meaningful to her than, say, Shakespeare? And do translations of literature produced abroad, without appropriate accompanying notes, really express the intricacies contained in the original? How are teachers who incorporate this kind of literature able to appear progressive without making significant curricular or instructional changes? How might such a presentation make English material appear the "norm" or "model" form of literature?

Relevance in cultural struggle: How do elements as presented in the sections above reflect the presence of cultural struggle within the classroom? How do these struggles represent or resemble struggles we read about in the newspapers or hear about in the nightly news? How does the teacher unwittingly and potentially contribute to the advantage of the dominant group in terms of devaluing cultural capital of other groups? What has the term *multicultural* come to mean for teachers, parents, researchers, and students in everyday practice?

From practice to praxis: As you consider the "negatives" discussed above, what opportunities do you see for challenging or shifting the categorizations as discussed? How did the journaling contribute to the teacher's realization of the situation as perceived by the student? How could this practice be extended to assist students to realize the power relationships in play? Does the teacher have a responsibility to change the literary selections? If so, should she replace the overseas sources or add others from the United States?

The introduction of literature into any classroom, but especially a foreign language classroom, can be a powerful motivational factor. Even complex literary genre information can be simplified in ways to make it accessible to students at the earliest levels of language instruction (Osborn 1998). But it is quite relevant to remember the caution of Wong (1993) in regard to comparative literary instructional practice:

A key instructional means of eliciting insight being comparison and contrast, at every turn we need to decide what to compare a marginalized literature to, and to what end. If this is done from a fallacious assumption of one's impartiality, however well-intentioned, the purpose of broadening the curriculum, namely, to honor the articulation of previously suppressed subjectivities, will be seriously undermined. (112)

Critical reflection enables the teacher to explore how impartial such presentations are. And just as the struggles in defining a society's literary past can be beneficial to contemporary students, the world of the school in terms of power relationships can be illustrative as well.

HOME ECONOMICS

Detached description: A male student claims that home economics is "girls' stuff," to which his female teacher responds with a brief rebuke. As she explains that he is simply vocalizing a sexist conceptualization of domestic roles, the student then queries, "Then why are there no male home ec teachers?"

Relevance for the classroom: How are teaching positions filled with regard to gender? Is it theoretically possible to have a male home economics teacher, and if so, what prevents more principals or personnel managers from employing them? Does the gender or ethnicity of a teacher lend a level of credibility to the subject matter? Are certain subjects more likely to have built-in gender or other bias in terms of instruction? How might these biases be reflected in the curriculum, the textbooks, or the theories and assumptions used to guide practice?

Relevance in society: Are the topics covered in traditional home economics courses still considered the domain of females? Are such conceptualizations reinforced as students see role models in teaching positions who are primarily female? What might be the response of a conservative (or liberal) community at having a male teacher of home economics? Where might one find males working in food service or clothing manufacturing positions? How do these positions differ in societal status from those related positions occupied by females?

Relevance in cultural struggle: If we assume that gender bias continues to be quite rampant in the professional and social world of the United States, in which ways does the dominant cultural capital value reflect such assumptions? Are there other elements of cultural struggle, such as the "glass ceiling," that contain the same patterns of exclusion?

From practice to praxis: Would simply hiring more males ameliorate the difficulties described? How could teachers currently in practice point students to other role models who would challenge existing stereotypes? Could certain television shows be used to highlight popular images? How have they evolved, and how have they not changed?

Kate Rousmaniere (1997) has noted, in regard to the history of women in the teaching profession, that

> While men were praised as professionals, women teachers were
> seen as merely fulfilling their "natural" attribute of caring for chil-
> dren. Mid-nineteenth-century common school reformers had
> supported the feminization of the teaching force. . . . Over time,
> the image of the moral and ever-patient woman teacher grew to be
> central to the cultural identity of the occupation. (40)

The politics of male and female differences in the school and workplace
is, in fact, quite widely recognized (see, for example, Apple 1995;
Giroux 1997b). And differences in the ways language is used by males
and females have become increasingly popularized (see Tannen 1994).

Again, though, foreign language classrooms have almost never addressed gender differences in the use of language. Presentation of colors in foreign language classrooms, for example, could draw attention
to the variety of colors females find as they enter the marketplace for
clothing and how these color schemes differ from those of male shoppers, and what kind of names of colors shoppers find in automobile
showrooms, for example. The use of language to create market appeal,
and a comparison and contrast of language patterns between males and
females, would be an appropriate, and politically insightful, point of departure within the language classroom.

I realize that some teachers work in contexts where it is currently difficult to realize the potential of a classroom culture built on insights
from critical reflection. The increasing use of standards in educational
planning and practice seems to interfere with an opportunity to experi-
ment with both curriculum and instruction. However, in challenging
these contemporary principles and practices, we can bring the classrooms closer to any regulative ideal.

QUESTIONS FOR REFLECTION

As you work through these examples of critical reflection, are there
   other issues that you would want to consider in the cases given?

Does the five-point pattern of analysis provide you with enough elements
   of coverage? Do you find yourself wanting to add or skip a certain
   category? What alternate patterns of analysis might you suggest?

TEACHING TO STANDARDS

Detached description: A teacher of science complains that "teachable
moments" seem to be a thing of the past because all of her time is taken

up with preparing students for standardized tests and following the curriculum standards prescribed by the state. Other teachers accuse her of being "burned out" and she sometimes wonders what ever became of her energy and the excitement she and her students found in discovery.

Relevance for the classroom: What are the programmatic objectives of having all teachers follow standards? Do national standards ensure that students in very different systems will obtain more equitable educational experiences? Do standards for curriculum affect a nation's ability to quantify successes of teachers? How accurate are standardized tests at measuring the teacher's ability to present the information mandated by standards in the classroom effectively? What role do standards play in keeping parallel courses at similar points in the textbook? How are textbooks related to prescribed curricular standards?

Relevance in society: Do the assumptions of production related to standards fit appropriately both as a business and educational metaphor? Should business frameworks be used to drive educational practice? Should models we use for education, nurturing, and so on, be used to guide successful businesses? What do production metaphors in education enable the business world to do in relation to effective hiring? In what ways have teachers become managers of students and behavior rather than intellectuals and cultural workers?

Relevance in cultural struggle: How do schools balance the demands of preparing students for the workplace with the ideals of a well-rounded education? How do the values and practices of certain segments of the population make their ways into these areas? How do teachers and students resist the imposition of standards of curricula or behavior? What role does this resistance play in the establishment or reproduction of social orders?

From practice to praxis: How can a teacher challenge the ideas that shape our national beliefs regarding standards? How can a teacher lead students to understand the power implications of their consent? What avenues of reform exist?

Standards for foreign language learning have been implemented in large part because of the work of professional organizations seeking to keep the profession on a par with other disciplines. Though typical arguments in favor of standards point to the ability of such frameworks to unite curricula nationwide and provide effective education for all, critical pedagogues point out that they can, and do, achieve just the opposite (see Apple 1996).

Similarly, by assuming that the teacher, the school, or the student is at fault when standards do not work, Apple (1995) explains that the state is "exporting the crisis," or allowing the educational program, not the societal power constellations underlying it, to take the blame for inequity. Yet as Anyon (1997) asserts, the role of the school in reproducing inequality can be quite effectively traced to numerous other economic, political, and cultural factors at work within the community and the state.

FOREIGN LANGUAGE CLASSROOMS

How do we approach the foreign language classroom in terms of critical reflection? It might be tempting to claim that we, as foreign language teachers, do not need to worry about the political struggles outside the classroom. We teach only language. The nuts and bolts of language use, vocabulary and grammar, are our objectives. Cultural blurbs are not really the focus of our lessons; therefore, we should just alter them a bit to reflect more adequately the changing demographics. Hopefully, some of you have begun to reject the idea that our classrooms are politically neutral and are embracing the tenets, if not also the process, of critical reflection.

How will critical reflection in the foreign language classroom resemble the examples above? At this point I would like to return to the five-point model and briefly describe aspects of foreign language instruction that should be of particular concern to practitioners.

Detached description: Teachers should attempt to provide in their descriptions as many viewpoints as can reasonably be assigned to students, teachers, or administrators. Avoid simply assuming that the administration is the "bad guy or girl," and resist reducing descriptives to statements that hide agents involved. "The principal instructs me" is better than "I am required to," and "The curriculum guide indicates" seems to ignore the fact that people wrote the guide. Attempt to identify interrelationships among the various agents involved, as their cultural frameworks will be relevant to continued and in-depth analysis.

Relevance for the classroom: Almost every action in a classroom is tied to some assumption about language, culture (in the traditional language classroom sense), education, or human psychology. Attempt to frame the description within these areas. For example, why is the passive voice important to the language? How is the passive used in the target language compared to English (if the target language is not English)? What is important about presenting the most complex material later in a semester? Continue to list as many assumptions as possible as part of the classroom analysis.

Relevance in society: In the broader U.S. society, and in the local community in which you teach, how do people view the elements discussed above? Is the grammar viewed as difficult, the vocabulary as novel, and the speakers as cultured and exotic or a threat to domestic security? Are the issues involved in language learning and acquisition inappropriately reduced in ways that disguise the difficulty of the endeavor? What kind of value is placed on these various aspects?

Relevance in cultural struggle: Since we are discussing language education within a linguistically diverse society, this analysis can be quite complex. Assume that you have a dominant culture and subordinate cultures within the United States. Assume that you have, as well, dominant and subordinate cultures within the other nations that speak the target language. Assume that speakers of the language in the United States may or may not be members of the dominant culture of the other nation, and as a result, may have conflicting stances. Their cultural capital may well represent the dominant one in the target culture, but a subordinate one locally. How do the cultures of other nations differ and come into conflict as presented in the classroom, and how does the foreign language learning environment assign value to each? Moreover, within the United States setting, how are these struggles reduced or essentialized so as to create a virtual two-dimensional concept of the target culture(s)? How then is the dominant culture of the United States, explicitly or implicitly, assigned greater value?

From practice to praxis: In challenging ideology or consent, the issues at hand in a foreign language class can be many. Certainly, questions related to how one defines oneself or others, how language is classified, or how multilingualism is perceived in the community could all be factors. As to consent, the role of language education in obtaining the benefits of the "good life" would provide many examples for students.

It should be noted that this particular form of critical analysis will take much practice before one becomes comfortable with it. In fact, one should always seek to challenge the examinations themselves and to allow for any "formula" to evolve. It is imperative to note, given the premise that we are educators, that we arrive at an unavoidable conclusion: A failure to address the issues highlighted through critical reflection on foreign language education in a democratic society, consisting of students possessing such diverse cultural capital, is tantamount to professional malpractice. The discipline of language education must enter the new millennium completely appreciating the gravity of our endeavor and most respond in a manner reflecting the best traditions of our profession.

QUESTIONS FOR DISCUSSION

Which reasons do language teachers give for wanting their students to learn "foreign" languages?

In which ways can critical reflection also contribute to these goals?

Chapter 5

The *Foreignness* Agenda

When defining an agenda for foreign language education in the United States, one would be hard-pressed to cite language proficiency. Such a claim is misleading and naive, and if true, would mean that the profession could be accused of incompetence at levels unheard of in American education. Imagine if students in math classes, at best, were able to recognize numbers up to the billions and could only recite the FOIL method of multiplication and the Pythagorean Theorem. If math students could not add, subtract, multiply, or divide in problems beyond those they had memorized, our society would be in serious trouble. It is probably true that our success record in language education has put the country in an equally precarious position (Simon, 1980).

If one appropriates the perspective afforded by critical educational studies, however, it becomes logical to consider that *foreignness*, or the ideological construction of an extra-national language identity in service of the dominant culture, is an agenda at which some success has been evident. Remembering that critical theorists reject the claim that students have not learned simply because educational programs seem to fail, one can see that the failure of an educational program (in this case foreign language education) may in fact represent a success in terms of hegemony.

In this chapter, we will apply the process of critical reflection discussed in Chapter Four to the foreign language classroom. You, the reader, are encouraged, however, not to limit yourself to a formula. The suggestions for critical reflection I have made can become as limiting as they may be liberating. Redefine the boundaries of inquiry as you see the need to do so, with an eye toward examining the effects of the schooling process on the student, the society, the teacher, and the best ideals of education.

Curriculum guides, which are sometimes called "standards," "outcomes," "frameworks," "course descriptions," and "course catalogs," can be a powerful source for a critical analysis of foreign language education. Though definitions of culture, language, foreign, and American are often vague and even contradictory, curriculum guides typically acknowledge the connection between language, culture, people, and society. They may indicate benefits of language study including enhancing cross-cultural awareness, preparation for life in a global community or multilingual/multicultural society, and the ability to analyze cultural differences or cultural influences on behavior.

Perhaps no single type of curricular item or document has been the subject of more scrutiny than the textbook. This trend is not without merit, for the textbook is often, beyond the teacher, the single most influential element in determining what happens in the classroom. Byram and Esarte-Sarries (1991), for example, assert that

Teachers use the textbook as their syllabus guidelines in the day-to-day planning of lessons, most evidently with respect to which language to introduce but also by extension with respect to what information to give pupils. They may rely entirely on the textbook or they may extend and elaborate, using their own materials or recounting their own experience. In principle they would decide independently what language and culture to introduce—provided that by the end of the course they had prepared pupils adequately for examinations. In practice, however, the order of introduction of topics in classes observed was determined by following the textbook, a system which ensures that parallel classes cover the same ground. This is normal practice in most schools. (173)

Apple and Christian-Smith (1991) explain further:

Texts are really messages to and about the future. As part of a curriculum, they participate in no less than the organized knowledge system of society. They participate in creating what a society has recognized as legitimate and truthful. They help set the canons of truthfulness and, as such, also help re-create a major reference point for what knowledge, culture, belief, and morality really *are*. (4)

But, one might argue, is not the very nature of studying another language going to lead to a better understanding of those who speak that language? Not necessarily, as Brosh (1997) has shown that textbooks used in Arabic classes in Israel present a "partial, subjective, and unbalanced" view of the Arab society (311). Similarly, foreign language textbooks in the United States can reflect messages with other agendas (see Mason and Nicely 1995; Ruiz 1987; Villa 1996; Wieczorek 1994). And as Kramsch (1993) reports,

American foreign language textbooks represent an educational culture that has its own agenda, and that is often more concerned about promoting American values of non-discrimination, non-sexism, religious tolerance, and physical health than about giving an authentic representation of the foreign culture. Pluralism is often the middle solution, that only thinly conceals a conservative, ethnocentric pedagogy. (228)

Kramsch goes on to explain that the mere presentation of cultural information, devoid of guidance to the student of appropriate techniques of contrast and synthesis, may risk "perpetuating the belief that beyond communication what really counts is only one's own way of life and system of thought" (228). As Rothstein (1991) points out,

The teacher, wishing to raise the consciousness of students, might engage them in a learning experience that helps them to cope with their own experiences. In order to do so, the teacher must find a way to avoid using this language of oppression. One approach could be to make students aware just how approximate knowledge of social reality is transformed into language. This could be done by studying how textbooks and spoken language signify reality and then listing the many features of observed situations that are omitted from these communications. (111)

Contemporary foreign language textbooks resemble large behe-moths, burdened by the weight of additions of material to please the teacher who wants to highlight grammatical items, another who wants to follow a communicative approach, and a profession intent on follow-ing a well-intentioned path to an acceptance of cultural diversity. The amount of visual "noise" generated on one page of text can leave one in a state of sensory overload. Bright, colorful pictures, helpful charts, study tips, and cultural notes are squeezed into every available space in the text.

There has also been a tremendous increase in the inclusion of cul-tural awareness material in the textbook. Whereas texts from the late seventies and early eighties typically included cultural information as supplementary material, the more contemporary texts proclaim that culture and language are inseparable. Appropriately, the textbooks have included the rhetoric characteristic of multicultural educational initia-tives. However, many stress that cultural understanding will come about as a natural result of comparing and contrasting cultural differ-ences, yet none explain precisely why this would be the case. Since there is compelling evidence to suggest that comparison and contrast may contribute to a sense of *foreignness*, however, the lack of a justification is particularly troubling (see Byram 1989).

To illustrate the inconsistencies one can find on the matter, let us consider the way several curriculum guides address the issue of cultural learning. New Jersey's state guide, for example, notes that learning cul-ture "is the process of examining, exploring, experiencing, and reacting to both the lifestyle and the accomplishments in the arts and sciences of the target language community" (New Jersey State Department of Education 1992, 11). Newark's local guide, however, posits that "for-eign languages and cultures have permeated all aspects of our contem-porary American life" (Newark Board of Education 1994, n.p.). Phoenix students of foreign language are called on to recognize the ex-istence of universal human values as a result of the study of language and culture (Phoenix Union High School District 1993), and Florida's guide asserts that "the interdependence of language and culture is a fairly new concept which has been extensively studied by sociolin-guists" (State of Florida Department of State 1996, 43).

Even understanding foreign language learning is subject to how one conceives the object of study. California defines foreign language as fol-lows: "The term *foreign language* is used here to denote any system of communication that is unfamiliar to students; for example Russian, Japanese, and German, among others" (California Department of Education 1989, 1). Nebraska, similarly, defines foreign language learning as "the perception, acquisition, organization, and storage of linguistic forms and cultural meanings of a language other than the learner's native language" (Nebraska Department of Education 1996, 128). Reflecting the confusion in distinguishing between ESL and foreign language instruction, California includes English as a second language (ESL) instruction within its guide, whereas Nebraska and many others do not.

Many foreign language texts include an opening section detailing the benefits of foreign language study. Typically, these pages refer to the numerous cities and rivers of the United States that have names originating from the language. Others cite historical connections to the United States, while some point out that many Americans trace their heritage to people who spoke the foreign language. This excerpt from *Komm mit!* (Winkler 1995) serves as a standard example:

Can you guess how many Americans trace all or part of their ethnic background to Germany, Austria, or Switzerland?—10 million? 30 million? 50 million? If you guessed 50 million, you were close! Forty-nine million people, or about 20% of the population, reported that they were at least partly of German, Swiss, or Austrian descent. Germans were among the earliest settlers in the United States. . . .

Everywhere, there are reminders of those early settlers: towns such as Hanover, North Dakota; Berlin, Wisconsin. . . .

Many traditions, such as the Christmas tree and the Easter bunny, as well as many words and phrases, like *pumpernickel, noodle, wurst, dachshund,* and *kindergarten* and those "typically American" foods such as hamburgers, pretzels, and frankfurters were brought over by German-speaking immigrants and have become part of our everyday life and language. . . .

Perhaps German will play an important role in your future. Many exciting jobs and careers require knowledge of a foreign language, and many employers consider it to be a great asset. (10)

Our Latin Heritage, on the other hand, refers to its value to the educated elite in society:

About eighty percent of the English vocabulary used by educated Americans is derived, directly or indirectly, from the Latin language. Throughout the Middle Ages, Latin was an international language. Until almost modern times it was the language of schools and scholars. Even in our day no person can claim to be fully educated without some knowledge of Latin culture. (Hines 1981, xiv)

French textbooks echo the emphasis on cultural contributions and employment benefits:

Francophone (French-speaking) cultures continue to make notable contributions to many fields, including art, literature, movies, fashion, cuisine, science, and technology. . . .

Being able to communicate in another language can be an advantage when you're looking for employment in almost any field. As a journalist, sportscaster, hotel receptionist, tour guide, travel agent, buyer for a large company, lawyer, engineer, economist, financial expert, flight attendant, diplomat, translator, teacher, writer, interpreter, publisher, or librarian, you may have the opportunity to use French in your work. (d'Usseau and DeMado 1996, 4)

Surprisingly, though, even when the topic at hand seems to necessitate that the textbook address the domesticity of linguistic diversity, *foreignness* still becomes the order of the day. In an introductory chapter entitled *¡Bienvenidos a San Antonio!*, for example, the opening dialogue is prefaced with the following: "In San Antonio, Chris Pearson meets a new *exchange student*, David, as they enter school" (Galloway, Joba, and Labarca 1998, 5, italics added). Certainly, if Chris were to speak to a U.S. citizen in Spanish, the dialogue would not be less authentic. Given the number of Spanish-speaking U.S. citizens in Texas and elsewhere, such an exchange would be both appropriate and authentic.

The majority of textbooks for foreign language classes focus on the idea of multicultural awareness as one of the most important reasons for studying a foreign language. Yet even those passages that speak of acceptance on one level can assign citizens in the United States who speak languages other than English the label of "foreign": "We want students to get to know what Spanish-speaking young people are like and to develop a feel for the everyday life in the *foreign* culture" (Cazabon et al. 1990, T11, italics added). Valette and Valette (1984), for example, encourage students by claiming that

> The study of Spanish is important for several other reasons. Language is part of culture. In learning a language, you learn not only how other people express themselves, but also how they live and what they think. It is often by comparing ourselves with others, by investigating how we differ and how we are similar, that we begin to learn who we really are. (iii)

As we compare ourselves with others, though, the danger exists that a concept of *foreignness* begins to be juxtaposed with the realities of *whiteness*.

In effect, by assuming that all non-English languages are somehow related to that which is foreign, language educational endeavors serve to reinforce a language identity by default. Though attempts to declare English an official language are often challenged, within the realm of common sense the national and official languages of the United States are both, and only, English. Nondominant language speakers are thereby marginalized as the media of their expression take on a devalued position. A student who chooses to adopt the view of the dominant culture, therefore, is often put in a position of assimilating linguistically. Further, those students who speak American English as a native language are firm in their beliefs that English is *the* language of the United States.

Further analysis of curricula reveals assumptions about native speakers of non-English languages in the United States context. For example, if one took curriculum guides and textbooks available in the United States as a whole, American Sign Language, it would appear, both is and is not a foreign language. Similarly, Native American languages are not considered "foreign" in Oklahoma, but Native Alaskan languages would seem to be "foreign" in Fairbanks.

The confusion regarding what *foreignness* is, however, should not be regarded as a conceptual stalemate. Defining what *foreignness* is can, and often is, accomplished by default. In other words, the foreign language curricula and textbooks may create the framework of *foreignness* by showing what it is not. At this point, I want for you to begin the analysis.

Consider, for instance, the following definitions based on Ohio's guide (Ohio Department of Education 1996) alone:

foreign languages: languages other than English (8)

target culture: the culture of the people who speak the target language (95)

target language: the language that is being taught or learned (95)

home (local) culture: the American culture (93)

How do these definitions reflect discourse common within the foreign language profession or classroom? How do they reflect the attitude of the dominant culture? If in the performance objectives, students are asked to compare aspects of the home and target cultures, how do these definitions serve to define *foreignness*? Consider the following argumentation:

If foreign = non-English speaking;

Target culture = foreign culture;

Home culture ≠ target culture; and

Home culture = American culture; then

American culture ≠ target culture = culture of non-English speakers.

In other words, the American culture is the culture of English speakers. This argument is logically fallacious, but it is not the soundness of the argument that is at issue. The reflection of how U.S.-Americans define what constitutes *foreignness* is germane. Consider now some alternate examples, and begin to follow the pattern of critical reflection, except for the final section (Practice to Praxis), which will be the focus of Chapter 6.

EXAMPLES OF ENGLISH LANGUAGE/AMERICAN SYNONYMY

One way in which language education practices in the United States at present contribute to a conceptualization of *foreignness* is a tendency to treat the classification "American" and the medium of the English language as though they were somehow the same. Indeed, there is nothing un-American about Spanish, French, German, or virtually any other language one can name.

Detached description(s): One claim within a curricular document reads as follows:

> A student of Arabic might come to understand that the terms for *host* and *guest* imply more social obligations in the Middle East than they do in the United States. (California Department of Education 1989, 5)

Relevance for the classroom: Oftentimes, students do not realize that when terms are translated, important facets of their meanings are lost. Language teachers, therefore, tend to stress the levels of meaning inherent in terms related to social custom.

Relevance in society: Understanding the obligations attached to social interactions is important when one is in a foreign land. Also, when one from a foreign land is in the United States, it is helpful to know these distinctions.

Relevance in cultural struggle: The connotations in language are inherent in the linguistic code, not in location. Actually, the terms for *host* and *guest* imply more obligations *in Arabic*, not just in the Middle East. The ideological assumptions underlying statements such as the one above seem to be either that everyone speaks English in the United States, or that Arabic customs are somehow "foreign."

Detached description: A curriculum guide contains the following objective:

> The students will demonstrate how non-verbal communications of Italian-speaking persons and Americans differ by preparing short skits. (Newark Board of Education 1994, n.p.)

Relevance for the classroom: Why are gestures and other nonverbal forms of communication important in an Italian classroom?

Relevance in society: How do forms of communication, both verbal and nonverbal, contribute to social interaction in a multicultural setting?

Relevance in cultural struggle: How are the categories of Italian-speaking person and American assumed to be different in the example above?

Detached description: Two passages from texts and curriculum guides follow:

Have them [students] draw similarities and differences between the Spanish-speaking world and the United States. (Gutiérrez, Rosser, and Rosso-O'Laughlin 1997, 15)

Spanish names are, of course, different from American names. (Wald 1991, 28)

Relevance for the classroom: Why are these forms of comparison and contrast utilized in a language classroom?

Relevance in society: How are descriptions of us and them used in society?

Relevance in cultural struggle: How do the examples above seem to treat English-language and "American" as synonymous?

QUESTIONS FOR REFLECTION

Consider the following passages, again taken from textbooks. How might you critically analyze them?

1. When a Hispanic person says *Tengo novio (novia) (I have a boy-friend/girlfriend)*, it implies a much more formal relationship than in the United States. (Jarvis et al. 1989, 83)

2. Sometimes the names of the nationality and the language are the same or similar:

   un muchacho *español*
   una muchacha *española*   } Hablan *español*

   Sometimes they are different:

   un señor *norteamericano*
   una señora *norteamericana*   } Hablan *inglés*
   (Wald 1991, 379)

EXAMPLES OF GEOGRAPHIC FRAGMENTATION

A second tendency of language education practice is to speak of the United States as divided into areas that are either linguistically diverse or not diverse. Further, there is a common association between native speakers of non-English languages and their "homelands," though they may indeed have been born in the United States.

Detached description: From curricular documents and textbooks, one can read: "Italian-American culture is another variation of Italian culture" (Newark Board of Education 1994, n.p.). From a learning scenario entitled "Cultural Connection Collaboration" "students write to regions in the target language country(ies) asking about holiday celebrations" and prepare a book including information about "how the target culture's traditions are practiced in Nebraska" (Nebraska Department of Education 1996, 91).

Relevance for the classroom: Why is it important to understand how cultural traditions are often associated with foreign lands?

Relevance in society: How are cultural traditions the source of both rich diversity and common misunderstanding?

Relevance in cultural struggle: Which cultural traditions are treated as though they were "100% American," though they, too, are tied to other countries? Whose traditions are they?

Detached description: An objective for a foreign language class: "When we have completed the first unit, you will be able to . . . recognize how Hispanic names differ from those in the United States (Babb, Mendes, and Entzi 1996, 1).

Relevance for the classroom: Why do we have our students look in phone books and other places for German-, Spanish-, or French-sounding names?

Relevance in society: What is the importance of a person's name in terms of identification and social interaction?

Relevance in cultural struggle: How are the sounds of names used in a discriminatory fashion?

Detached description: A description of students in a level two class is as follows: "Phonological and grammatical errors are fewer than in level one, but still occur frequently enough to mark the student distinctly as a foreigner" (Cranston [Rhode Island] Public Schools 1989, 23).

Relevance for the classroom: Why do we set expectations for language learners after one year at a level below that of native speaker?

Relevance in society: How are linguistic limitations viewed in society? Do those perceptions differ based on the language one is proficient in?

Relevance in cultural struggle: How are language barriers utilized in the process of social discrimination?

QUESTIONS FOR REFLECTION

Consider the following excerpts in light of geographic fragmentation. How do they seem to locate linguistic and cultural diversity?

> The learner will use a globe, map, and other reference materials to locate and name at least one country or local neighborhood where people speak the target language. (Ohio Department of Education 1996, 31)

> Cultural proficiency should relate to the target culture, both past and present, as found throughout the world and in the United States. (Cranston Public [Rhode Island] Schools 1989, 8)

> What are some similarities and differences between who is considered a friend in a Spanish-speaking country and in the United States? What could you expect to occur if you became friends with someone in a Spanish-speaking country? (Met, Sayers, and Wargin 1996, 40)

EXAMPLES OF PATERNALISTIC EMPOWERMENT

A common theme of language learning in the United States is that the process is good not only for the student, but also for the native speakers of the language. Often couched in rhetoric of empowerment, the problem of a perceived deficiency can remain.

Detached description: An advantage of studying American Sign Language is stated to be the following:

> Students without a hearing impairment may enroll in those [ASL] classes. When they do, the state's hearing-impaired students become less isolated from the social and economic mainstream. Their confidence and self-esteem increase. (California Department of Education 1989, 12)

Relevance for the classroom: Why do teachers of foreign languages often tell students the benefits of learning a foreign language?

Relevance in society: How are speakers of "foreign" languages marginalized in society?

Relevance in cultural struggle: How could depictions of non-English speakers in foreign language classes contribute to a perception that English is a superior language in the United States?

Detached description: Another advantage to language study is indicated as follows:

> [S]tudents' [whose first language is "foreign"] self-esteem is often raised when they are given a chance to increase their competency in a language spoken at home (and when they realize that competency is valued by a respected educational institution). (California Department of Education 1989, 12)

Relevance for the classroom: Again, why do foreign language teachers promote their subject by pointing out its relevance to the "real world?"

Relevance in society: How does the credibility of an educational institution translate to prestige for societal issues or causes?

Relevance in cultural struggle: How do educational institutions systematically devalue or value the language skills of individuals in the United States?

QUESTIONS FOR REFLECTION

How do the following citations reflect the idea that speakers of non-English languages are struggling with a deficiency?

[Learners will] prepare short talks on what accommodations are made in their everyday lives for the Italian-speaking people who cannot speak English. (Newark Board of Education, 1994, n.p.)

The training of non-hearing-impaired students in Sign Language would assist in efforts to make a wider range of experiences available to the hearing-impaired. (South Carolina State Board of Education 1993, 14)

For the bilingual student, second language acquisition is easier when children come to school knowing that their language and culture are just as important as English. . . . For bilingual students such a message validates their heritage, language, and culture and sets the stage for a successful school experience.[1]

EXAMPLES OF ECONOMIC TRAJECTORIES

Often, native speakers of non-English languages are depicted in ways that presume to relegate them to certain jobs in lower socioeconomic strata. This process reflects a stereotype contributing to *foreignness*.

Detached description: An advantage of language education is reported to be as follows:

> As American society becomes more culturally diverse, so does the work force—and the plant manager or personnel manager who can communicate in more than one language has an advantage. (South Carolina State Board of Education 1993, 3)

Relevance for the classroom: How are the interests of business represented within the foreign language classroom?

Relevance in society: Why do employers want their managers to possess language skills in the United States?

Relevance in cultural struggle: How are the benefits of studying foreign languages linked to a student's expected employment future? What might those students anticipate in regard to the native languages of their employees?

Detached description: Within a discussion of linguistic diversity, one document contains the following:

> In some communities there is great fluctuation in [language minority] student populations due to the arrival of new immigrants or to the closing of a manufacturing plant.[2]

Relevance for the classroom: How do language classes support the relevance of their subject by pointing out the native speakers of the language within the community?

Relevance in society: How is the possession of English skills tied to levels of economic success in the United States?

Relevance in cultural struggle: How do students perceive the marketable skills of people in their community who speak "foreign" languages?

CHANGING LABELS

Finally, it is important to note the expanding terminology used in the United States to refer to foreign languages and native speakers. The language is often depicted as a tool, the native speakers as resources. In one state, for example, the term "Drillmasters" was changed to Native Languages Resources (NLR) to describe native speakers of the "foreign language" who were employed for a variety of linguistic reinforcement activities in the classroom. Several texts give teachers the suggestion that, to help their students increase their awareness of *foreign* culture, they should take them to local *ethnic* restaurants. This synonymy is troubling due to the equivalent status given *ethnic* and *foreign*, especially when one considers which languages are taught in the United States.

Detached description: Within curricular documents used in the United States, the following terms are used synonymously with *foreign* in the way that they function: languages other than English, second languages, non-native languages, target language, other languages, advanced languages, world languages, and modern and classical (when taken together) languages.

Relevance for the classroom: Why are foreign language teachers looking for alternatives to the marker *foreign* to describe their subjects?

Relevance in society: How does terminology play an important role in public perception? Give additional examples.

Relevance in cultural struggle: How is "political correctness" a way to avoid seeming discriminatory while at the same time allowing some to continue practices that discriminate?

CONCLUSION

In this chapter, I have led you through a series of brief passages taken from foreign language textbooks and curriculum guides nationwide. Though not intended as an indictment against language educators, I have attempted to point out that the concepts underlying an ideology supporting *foreignness* remain in place both within and beyond the term *foreign* itself. Simply changing the descriptor of the subject, without challenging the underlying mental frameworks, will only result in a situation where, as Apple (1979) described, "historically outmoded, and socially and politically conservative (and often educationally disastrous) practices are not only continued, but are made to sound *as if they were actually more enlightened* and ethically responsive ways of dealing with children" (144, italics added).

The task of language educators in the twenty-first century must shift to reflect activity greater than moving away from cultural "otherness." As one language text explained,

There was a time when "culture" in the average French course meant providing information about the French Revolution, relating anecdotes from the lives of Molière and Napoléon, and assigning intensive map work to drill the major cities and rivers of France. Also included was a discussion of holidays and customs, especially where those could be considered quaint or odd. The basis of this approach to culture was the "otherness" of the speakers of the target language. Students were encouraged to think of speakers of French as foreigners—"Them"—people completely unlike the students themselves, either because of their remoteness in time, or because of the perceived oddity of their life styles.

Many of the things that were taught in the past—Culture with a capital C—still have their place in the curriculum, but primary importance now is given to helping students view the speakers of the target language as human beings with whom they have much in common." (Valdman et al. 1986, T25)

More than merely advocating the study of cultural similarities and differences, the critically reflective language educator acknowledges a responsibility to point out to students how language, language policies, language planning, and language education are used in discriminatory ways. Through this form of praxis, the teacher ceases pseudo-neutrality and begins to strive toward ends of social justice within the very space now used to marginalize native speakers of non-English languages.

QUESTIONS FOR DISCUSSION

Can you provide additional examples of the *foreignness agenda* as found in language textbooks, specifically geographic fragmentation, English/American synonymy or paternalistic empowerment?

At this point, which alterations to the methods of critical reflection presented here might you suggest? Which ones seem more effective? Less effective?

NOTES

1. Taken from the Massachusetts World Languages Framework, available online at www.doe.mass.edu.

2. Ibid.

Chapter 6

Transforming *Foreignness*

Having introduced the reader to the constructs employed in language classes that reinforce the idea of *foreignness* in terms of non-English languages within the United States, the focus of the text moves now toward praxis. I wish to distinguish practice, that is, what teachers do, from praxis, which is theory-informed practice. Further, in a critical sense, praxis must be emancipatory in orientation. Stated another way, the point of a critically reflective language teacher's practice is to facilitate the students' ability to perceive the ideological elements of language issues in society and in education.

The language teacher can accomplish these goals in terms of *foreignness* by challenging either the consent to relationships of dominance (by removing the sanction of either the oppressor or the oppressed), or by confronting the ideological constructs themselves. In this chapter, I will illustrate examples of both techniques as they can be executed within the language classrooms of the twenty-first century. These too should be seen as a genesis to future praxis. Incorporating the insights of critical pedagogy is challenging in an age of increased central prescriptiveness in education, but teachers have a significant history of such endeavors.

Irwin (1996) has identified a promising trend in contemporary U.S. education:

> For we are beginning to recognize again that teaching is a fundamentally moral enterprise. How we treat children who are different, how we deal with antisocial behavior, and how we decide what is to be taught are all essentially moral decisions. As moral agents, teachers must have enough control of their teaching to ensure that they cannot be forced to act against the interests of their students. (114)

Most experienced teachers will relate, however, that in fact they cannot be forced to act against what they consider to be the best interests of themselves, the community, or the students, as their own priorities would dictate. Teachers typically refer to the adage, "when that classroom door closes," and they proclaim their own veto power over any mandate, curricular, legal, administrative, or otherwise. Only challenges of moral or professional impropriety wield power to dissuade a teacher from exercising her or his own form of "academic freedom." It is this veto power over curricular mandates, both explicit and implicit, that can become part of any teacher education program desiring to move teachers from those who simply understand what is transpiring in relation to the sociological nature of schooling, to those who have the power to change it. As Wink (1997) has argued in regard to transformative models of lesson design,

> The fundamental belief that drives these classroom behaviors is that we must act; we must relate our teaching and learning to real life; we must connect our teaching and learning with our communities; we always try to learn and teach so that we grow and so that students' lives are improved, or for self and social transformation. . . . This new approach to teaching and learning challenges teachers to have complex pedagogical skills. (118)

Curricular nullification can be a tool of empowerment, and it operates as a socially transformative potential.

CURRICULAR NULLIFICATION

There has been some publicity given recently to a phenomenon that takes place in courtrooms known as jury nullification. In essence, the jury, for a variety of reasons, though aware of the legal mandates before them as applied to a particular case, chooses to disregard those issues and return a verdict that is inconsistent with the law as well as with the evidentiary findings. This provides a useful analogy for actions taken commonly by teachers in general, and foreign language teachers specifically.

Not only do students reject the explicit and implicit curricula, I would argue, but teachers sometimes do as well. In the case of foreign language teachers, for example, one may decide not to teach the subjunctive mood because it is too difficult or irrelevant for students. Along the same lines, I have known one teacher of French who refused to teach both the formal and familiar verb forms, arguing that students most likely will only use the formal form when meeting French-speaking adults, and he opted therefore to present only that form to the students.

Regardless of the accuracy of his claim, this teacher was engaged in the process of curricular nullification. Knowing that the curriculum mandates teaching both verb forms, and deciding not to, is nullifying the mandate. Curricular nullification is the result of action(s) or a failure to act by an educator, the effect of which stands in opposition to explicit or implicit curricular mandates or goals. Curricular nullification can be further analyzed utilizing several distinct "oppositions" that serve to demarcate its complex nature.

SUBTRACTIVE AND ADDITIVE CURRICULAR NULLIFICATION

Subtractive curricular nullification occurs when one fails to engage in behaviors that are curricularly and institutionally mandated, including omitting topics from the syllabus. The example of the teacher of French given above is subtractive. It is also relevant to contrast subtractive curricular nullification with modification. When a teacher modifies course content for a student with special needs, for example, that teacher is removing course content in hopes of meeting curricular mandates or goals. Subtractive curricular nullification, by definition, stands to contradict, oppose, and nullify objectives by virtue of an omission. It is important to note that some cases of subtractive curricular nullification would be unethical, and more extreme ones might actually constitute professional malpractice. For instance, a teacher of sex education who fails to provide students with information regarding sexually transmitted diseases could be accused of subtractive curricular nullification that is indeed malpractice.

Additive curricular nullification is the act of engaging in behaviors beyond those mandated in the curriculum, again with the intent of contradicting, opposing, or nullifying objectives. If a social studies teacher, when finishing a discussion on tolerance of diversity, closes with the comment, "And that's why the country has gone downhill," that teacher has engaged in additive curricular nullification. The unit was taught, but the addition of the comment was contradictory to curricular mandates. In a foreign language setting, if the hidden curriculum of the course includes a goal of keeping the target language and its associated culture "foreign," then a teacher who brings her or his students to see the presence of the language and culture in their own community, thus demonstrating its domesticity, is attempting to practice additive curricular nullification. Again, additive curricular nullification in extreme cases could be unethical or represent professional malpractice, as might be the case of a secondary teacher who brought underage students to a bar to discuss cultural differences in attitudes toward alcohol consumption.

ETHICAL AND UNETHICAL CURRICULAR NULLIFICATION

Curricular nullification can be ethical or unethical. Ethical behavior here refers to professionally recognized, appropriate behavior. Certainly that which constitutes ethical or unethical behavior changes and is often based on a power relationship as well. This fact notwithstanding, the qualification is relevant for the world of the practitioner (and researcher) who obviously could be terminated for unethical behavior.

Strike and Soltis (1992) assert,

> We believe that a kind of rational ethical thinking that goes beyond personal beliefs and values is essential both to professional ethics and to the moral education of all members of society. Ethics is a public as well as a personal matter. If we are correct, then it would seem to follow that teachers have a special obligation to help their students see and share the potential objectivity and rationality of ethical thinking so that we can all lead morally responsible lives together. (5)

Though curricular nullification as a phenomenon certainly involves choices based on individual belief systems, curricular nullification as a pedagogy must be based on that which is morally responsible and ethical.

DISSONANTAL AND HARMONIOUS CURRICULAR NULLIFICATION

Dissonantal curricular nullification is that which occurs in conflict with the agent's own value and belief system. The concept of cognitive dissonance, as outlined by Wicklund and Brehm (1976), is helpful in understanding the distinction discussed here:

> Any bit of knowledge that a person has about himself or the environment is a "cognition," or "cognitive element." . . . The relationship between two cognitive elements is *consonant* if one implies the other in some psychological sense. Psychological implication can arise from cultural mores, pressure to be logical, behavioral commitment, past experience, and so on. . . . If having cognition *A* implies having cognition *B*, a dissonant relationship exists when the person has cognitions *A* and the obverse or opposite of *B*. (2)

Though a detailed discussion of the theories and arguments related to cognition and dissonance is well beyond the purview of this analysis, the point to be gained here is simply that given one "cognitive element" or value, an act of curricular nullification may be psychologically implied by that element or may be its obverse or opposite.

As to the example at hand, if one teaches for the goals of social justice and discovers that a curriculum supports hegemony, an act of curricular nullification may be harmonious (consonance implies only cognitive consistency; the term used here includes values or other elements beyond "knowledge") or dissonantal. For some, all curricular nullification may be dissonantal. For another, all may be harmonious. This distinction is one of an internal check in much the same way ethical/unethical represents an external check.

INTENTIONAL AND CONSEQUENTIAL CURRICULAR NULLIFICATION

Finally, a distinction needs to be made briefly between curricular nullification as the result of intentional action or inaction and that which is caused by a seemingly unrelated action or set of actions. Causation is essential to establish a classification of curricular nullification as intentional or consequential. The clarification is needed to determine a basis of curricular nullification as a pedagogy, since it is the intentional form that can be included as part of a strategy of social activism. Though consequential curricular nullification may well further the ends that activists desire, because it is caused by unrelated action it does not constitute an effective strategic element of activism.

CURRICULAR NULLIFICATION AS SOCIAL ACTIVISM

Having identified characteristics and qualifications of curricular nullification, it becomes important to understand the relationship of each set to the agent of change and to the curricular mandates, both implicit, as in a hidden curriculum, and explicit. Figure 3 is a representation of this relationship.

Though the forms presented are all examples of curricular nullification, it is the intentional, harmonious, and ethical forms that can be utilized as a socially transformative potential and that should become part of the language teacher's pedagogical repertoire.

Curricular nullification should be incorporated into practice with the intent of challenging the boundaries of educational concepts and practices, and thus uncoupling various parts of the elements of the concept *foreignness* from the language and its speakers. By opposing any one or all of the component parts discussed in the previous chapter that contribute to the maintenance of hegemonic relationships, for example, curricular nullification begins to function in its capacity as a socially transformative potential.

Curricular nullification, when intentional, harmonious, and ethical, can have the effect of transformative action and meets the calls for emancipatory activism common to the literature of critical pedagogy. Since a large segment of the population will be in a foreign language class as part of the gatekeeping function for college admission, these students can learn to question their own consent to such ideas as "What does it mean to be an American?" or "Who can be considered a foreigner in the United States?" Critically reflective language teachers can add or remove elements from the curriculum, as professionally appropriate, in ways that support this endeavor.

Figure 3
Curricular Nullification and the Relationship to the Agent of Change

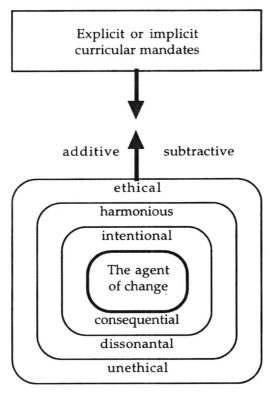

QUESTIONS FOR REFLECTION

How have you or your teachers added to textbooks or prescribed curricula to achieve goals you felt were important but seemingly ignored by those who plan for the course?

What element could be added to a course (a lesson, a film, a discussion) that would challenge the ideological underpinnings of geographic fragmentation?

How can students be made aware of their abilities not to consent to the *foreignness* agenda?

INTEGRATED/INTERDISCIPLINARY ACTIVITIES

Jacobs (1989) has produced an excellent volume on the development and implementation of interdisciplinary curricula. Within this text, Ackerman (1989) has pointed to a set of criteria that can be adapted for the purposes of language instruction: validity within the disciplines, validity for the disciplines, and validity beyond the disciplines. Understanding how these criteria are evaluated is prerequisite to utilizing such units in challenging *foreignness*.

When organizing an interdisciplinary unit, one should focus on an appropriate theme that will tie disciplines (for example, Spanish and history) together. The thematic approach to integrated, interdisciplinary activities provides the teacher with a conceptual "glue" and a point from which to proceed within the curricular framework (see Lonning, DeFranco, and Weinland 1998). The theme, however, must be more than simply a contrived connection between the two disciplines. Certainly, one could argue that the letter *i* provides a connection between Spanish and history, since both titles include it. A unit could then be developed that studies Spanish words beginning with *i* and historical figures or events that also begin with the letter *i*. Such a connection, however, is contrived. Ackerman stresses that the theme must be important to the individual discipline or field of study. Most language classes would not develop themes around the letter *i*, nor would history classes. The theme must be valid within the disciplines.

A second point is that the interdisciplinary theme must support the learning of other concepts in the individual disciplines. Indeed, a student of German and a student of history would both benefit from an understanding of how languages evolve. Language planning, for example, would touch on political issues of the Nazi era as it would demonstrate to language students that compound nouns in German are often officially replaced with simpler, more manageable words. This satisfies a criterion Ackerman refers to as validity for the disciplines.

Finally, the idea of validity beyond the disciplines is best summarized as a theme that allows students to look beyond the subjects involved to the world. A curriculum or lesson based on interdisciplinary elements must also give students a "metaconceptual bonus" (Ackerman 1989, 29; see also 27–30). Within this framework, one can begin to structure lessons that effectively challenge the *foreignness* agenda. Such an interdisciplinary unit could include the language and social studies or economics or other subjects, but I want to focus on units that incorporate the local community with its native speakers, conceptualized for purposes of unit development as a *discipline*.

Since the publication of the *Standards for Foreign Language Learning*, many scholars have sought to develop practical applications of the mandates contained within (Lafayette 1996). Overfield (1997) has appropriately pointed out the strength of "situating foreign language education within the literal and metaphorical spaces of our communities [to] emphasize the relevance of foreign languages in the contemporary world" (485). Her adaptation of models of community-based learning and communicative competence represents a skillful attempt at addressing the standard related to communities.

By the developing the units in the way that I propose, however, teachers and students can utilize the spaces afforded by critical reflection within our classrooms to challenge the ways in which *foreignness* has situated our particular educational endeavor in the national discourse. Teachers will utilize the community not as an object of study, but as a discipline, an authoritative body of knowledge.

If language teachers conceive the community of native language speakers as a discipline, then a more effective use of native speakers beyond the classroom can result. Simply going to an ethnic restaurant to experience "foreign" culture is not the most effective or appropriate use of the local community. Themes developed in the way I propose will more accurately reflect the relevance of cuisine within the native speaker community. It is doubtful that those speakers consider Italian or Mexican food, for example, as solely indicative of a connection to a foreign land. Instead, gathering at a meal or working in a restaurant has a meaning to the community members, is tied to other elements within the community, and can enable students to look at social interaction as reflective of many historical and sociopolitical relationships.

TOWARD AUTHENTIC EMPOWERMENT

By utilizing elements of both curricular nullification, to challenge the consent to the *foreignness* agenda, and instructional techniques such as the interdisciplinary unit, critically reflective language teachers can create classrooms that result in the authentic empowerment of native speakers within the community. By way of analogy, qualitative researchers recognize the need for the emic (insider's) perspective when reporting ethnographic research. Language classes must also seek to encourage students' understanding of native speakers within the community, not as *foreigners*, but in a manner more reflective of their actual community position.

Moreover, since many non-English-speaking citizens may still conceptualize their own position as "foreign," language teachers will need to address reasons such an ideology is in place as well. Additionally, since many immigrants come to the United States with preconceived notions of what it means to be American as expressed in their homelands,[1] the hegemony related to *foreignness* will need to be challenged for speakers of all languages in the United States.

As an example of such a unit, let us assume that a teacher of German and a teacher of history would like to illustrate the concept of political resistance. With two disciplines represented, we need to consider the third discipline of the language community. Native speakers engage in resistance as they refuse to assimilate linguistically. When speakers of Spanish, for example, refuse to allow employers to ban their language from the workplace and take those challenges to court, they are involved in resistance. When German speakers in the United States during the early twentieth century assimilated due to the hysteria in the country, their resistance was likely present, but unsuccessful. The theme of resistance might well be appropriate, but it should be evaluated in light of the criteria presented above.

Is resistance a theme that has validity for the disciplines of social studies, German, and for non-English speakers in the United States? In social studies it certainly does in American history. In a German language class, I would argue, it does as well. Many times students who take German do not have realistic understanding of the Nazi atrocities. In the past, I have had students who summed up their insight with a comment on how "the marching was cool," and others who attributed the viciousness of the regime to the German population as a whole. Though Goldhagen (1996) has argued that one cannot lay blame only on the Nazi party or the SS, there are also well-documented instances of resistance by Germans, notably in those groups referred to as the Red Orchestra and the White Rose.

The Red Orchestra, or *Rote Kapelle*, as it was known by the Gestapo, was a circle of smaller resistance groups in Germany that emerged in the late thirties, to be discovered in the summer of 1942. Arvid and Mildred Harnack (the latter an American) and Harro and Libertas Schulze-Boysen distributed anti-Nazi leaflets and communicated with Soviet intelligence in an attempt to oppose the National Socialist regime. The Harnack and Schulze-Boysen organization members were accused of being part of a Soviet espionage ring, and beginning in late

1942, sentences of death for over fifty members of the group were carried out by order of the Reich Military Court (Steinbach 1990).

At the University of Munich, meanwhile, siblings Hans and Sophie Scholl began to decry the deceit of the National Socialists and were instrumental in the distribution of leaflets at the university and throughout Germany. They were joined by classmates in their undertakings and were encouraged by one professor, Kurt Huber. While distributing flyers in the lecture hall one day, a building superintendent spied the Scholls and reported them to the Gestapo. The Scholls and many in the group known as the White Rose were executed for their actions.

Today, streets at the university are named in their honor and their sacrifice is remembered annually. The courage of their resistance is perhaps best explained by their sister, Inge:

> It was an instance in which five or six students took it upon themselves to act while the dictatorship was totally in control; in which they accepted the lonely burden of not being able to discuss these matters with their families; in which they took action even through the omnipotent state allowed them no room to maneuver; in which they acted in spite of the fact that they could do no more than tear small rifts in the structure of that state—much less blast out the cornerstones. . . . It is rare that a man is prepared to pay with his life for such a minimal achievement as causing cracks in the edifice of the existing order. (Scholl 1983, 103)

The stories of resistance can prove to be not only inspirational for students, but quite applicable to the struggles that elements of the population face today in a climate of increasing animosity toward linguistic diversity.

But now we should return to the question of validity for the discipline of native speakers within the community. As I write this, in New York City daily protests are staged against four police officers, who mortally wounded an unarmed West African immigrant by firing over forty bullets. In another part of the city, Americans who support the ethnic Albanians in Kosovo, and others who condemn NATO attacks, take to the streets for their voices to be heard. On Long Island, municipalities struggle with the question of whether to declare English the official language. Non-native speakers of English in these communities, as well, make their voices heard at town council meetings or in other appropriate forums. Though these issues are not all based solely on language, they do represent concerns of native-speaking communities, and thus resistance can be considered to have validity for the discipline.

Does the theme of resistance assist students in learning other concepts within the disciplines? Again, for social studies the answer should be affirmative. In German, though, one might challenge such an assertion. But understanding resistance can lead to an appreciation of how societies deal with loan words (as in the case of the Académie Française, for example), how language planning and political ends are interrelated (see Tollefson 1991, 1995), and how cultural struggles are present in language-related issues. Some vocabulary even evolves as a result of, or describes, resistance activities, such as the American English terms *sit-in*, *boycott*, and *strike*.

For language students to understand native-speaking cultures within the United States, studying the theme of resistance is helpful in analyzing other elements within the culture. How speakers view themselves and others, and how they interact cross-culturally can all be expected to have appropriate ties to resistance. Economic factors and dropout rates may also be tied to resistance activities (see Willis 1977). Thus we can claim that this theme has validity within the "native speaker community" discipline.

The final issue to determine is the concept of validity beyond the disciplines or the "metaconceptual bonus." If students begin to develop a recognition of the ways in which resistance plays into language, history, and the native-speaking culture of the United States, the school curriculum is closer to subjectification. In other words, its sociopolitical, historical, and economic bases begin to be exposed, and if properly encouraged, students will begin to expand their range of analysis beyond *foreignness* to other issues in all classes as well. This reality enables this theme to qualify as valid beyond the disciplines.

Having passed the tests of validity, the next step involves designing the unit. Lonning, DeFranco, and Weinland (1998) have advanced a theoretical model that is helpful to this end. They suggest that the place to begin (even before tests of validity) is with a local curriculum guide. Choosing objectives from the guide, teachers can then develop units that integrate the disciplines. Within the newest foreign language standards and guides, encouraging students to make connections to other subjects and to the native-speaking communities in the area is explicitly encouraged. Thus, the following hypothetical objectives or performance standards might apply:

The student will write a formal letter using the proper format.

The student will express likes and dislikes.

The student will give reasons for an opinion.

The student will demonstrate an awareness of diversity within the nation.

If a language teacher developed a unit around resistance and introduced students to the facts regarding resistance groups in Germany during the Nazi era (as a tie to history), a contemporary application of studying resistance in the language classroom could still be framed within communicative objectives. Students could practice, in the target language, writing a letter of protest, expressing a dislike, giving reasons for the opinion, and attempting to do so from the emic perspective of the native-speaking community. Language skills are being learned at the same time that the students become critically aware of language issues within their own society. Such a theme would likely be much more meaningful for our students than discussing how many chess players there are in Switzerland or the intricacies of school systems in other parts of the world. The cultural struggles surrounding languages and their speakers are identified, and *foreignness* is incrementally transformed.

QUESTIONS FOR REFLECTION

Brainstorm for some additional themes that would be appropriate both within the native-speaking communities of the United States and the language classroom.

Why do some native speakers of non-English languages commonly distinguish between "us" and "the Americans?"

TOWARD TRANSFORMING *FOREIGNNESS*

The young Appalachian wife, as the story goes, was talking with a friend while preparing dinner for her family and guests. The friend looked on inquisitively as the woman cut off both ends of a ham she was preparing to roast, and then put it into a large pan, which she placed into the hot oven. The friend asked, "Why did you cut off the ends?" "Hmmm. I don't know, my mother always did, replied the wife."

Later the wife called her mother, who told her that her own mother had also followed the procedure. Reaching her grandmother, the wife carried on the inquiry. "Why that's simple, dear," the octogenarian replied. "When I first married, our pan was too small for the whole ham to fit. I just never got out of the habit."

The story can serve as an allegory for the situation one finds in contemporary foreign language programs. The design of these programs has been similar for so many years that the genesis of many of our practices and the ideas guiding them has been lost. It is likely that this phenomenon is partially responsible for the multiple schisms within our profession. Bureaucratic cries of "scandal" for our alleged failure to produce communicatively competent speakers are not only misplaced, but also disguise the very source of that failure. We, as language education professionals, know quite well how languages can be learned, and if budgets and support were unlimited, we could quite effectively create a multilingual society. Unfortunately, such carte blanche is not likely to be granted.

The interests of the dominant, English-speaking culture would dictate that foreign language classes indeed fail at the endeavor to create a multilingual populace. Otherwise, the political voice that would be gained by speakers of non-English languages must certainly seem threatening to those who now hold power. English-only movements, California's decimation of bilingual education, and other debates regarding language use in public places are part of the same *foreignness* agenda. Language educators within the United States must recognize the nature of our own professional activity in this regard.

Therefore, the role of language education in the United States cannot rest any longer solely on the hope of learning a language in two to four academic years. Language educators who are critically reflective practitioners can begin the process of transforming *foreignness*. Language classes will need to encourage students to interact in meaningful ways with those whose cultures and languages seem to differ from their own; at the same time there must be a concerted institutional effort to educate all staff and students on the issues involved in linguistic and cultural diversity (Hamayan 1990; Milk, Mercado, and Sapiens 1992; Rigg and Allen 1989; Wong-Fillmore 1991a, 1991b). This cannot be a quick lecture on the virtues of tolerance. It must be a systematic, sustained educational effort designed to increase the awareness by each institutional member of his or her own prejudices, attitudes toward linguistic diversity, and educational implications of cultural differences. Language classrooms can become the central departure point in the school and local community for such education.

Multilingualism should be promoted through a variety of activities as a goal for all students. School-wide announcements could be in languages other than English, in addition to the typical English announcements. Signs, preferably official ones, could be printed in the various languages represented in the school. Activities highlighting linguistic and cultural diversity can be planned to involve the entire student population. And transforming *foreignness* will include challenging the disciplines that exist within language education itself.

It has always been perplexing to this author that English as a Second Language (ESL) and foreign language classes are treated as separate disciplines. ESL and foreign language classes and faculty could become a part of a new "World Language Department," with the ESL class being retitled American English. The advantages of this reorganization are compelling. Recognition of English language learners as being involved in the same process as their native-speaking counterparts would effectively challenge the stigma of remediation often attributed to ESL classes. The reorganization will allow for teachers of the two disciplines to share information, resources, and techniques. Students in both sets of classes can co-construct knowledge of the ways in which language functions within their community.

CONCLUSION

This text can only serve, at best, as a beginning to a reinvigoration of language teaching. I am of the firm opinion that teachers every day can discover applications of the discussion in this text that exceed in effectiveness any example I can give. In essence, the examples of curricular nullification and unit development point to a central goal. We must challenge the boundaries of educational discourse in foreign language education. We must move beyond treating the classroom as one culture that is somehow separate from its surrounding community and cultures. Language classrooms are not institutional think tanks for the study of static particles of linguistic information. They must become dynamic cultures of critical reflection geared toward equipping students with the necessary skills and insights for positive social change. These improvements in both theory and practice will move language classrooms in the U.S. democracy into the twenty-first century.

QUESTIONS FOR DISCUSSION

Brainstorm for activities that language teachers could include in their classes that would eliminate the walls that traditionally separate the disciplines of foreign language, English as a Second Language, and bilingual education. How could those activities be publicized so as to bring a greater community awareness to the issues of language diversity?

The role of teachers in reforming language education will be of utmost importance in the coming century. Discuss how teachers perceive their roles in the current system. What avenues do teachers have available for professional improvements?

How do standards and broadly administered tests hamper curricular reform?

NOTE

1. My gratitude is extended to C. J. Mellor for pointing out this facet of *foreignness*, personal communication, March 4, 1999.

Chapter 7

Toward a (Re)new(ed) Professional Vision

The *foreignness* agenda, as an expression of sociocultural distinctness growing out of a framework we have discussed as whiteness, cannot be easily assigned to the realm of language education in all instances. Certainly in terms of the classics, it seems difficult to argue that native speakers of Latin are not foreign to the United States, though ironically, Latin teachers correctly stress that the language is very much alive in the United States today (i.e., not a dead language). And though education in the Latin language has and should continue to have a place in language education, the exigencies of providing quality language education in the United States necessitate addressing the issues raised by critical reflection in world language education.[1] Our professional vision simply must continue to keep pace with the changing world around us. It is this same conviction that led to the development of standards for language learning, and that should now lead us to consider broadening our horizons even further. We must now move to and beyond a vision of transforming *foreignness*, to equipping students who will encounter the world of linguistic diversity in their own communities, not simply overseas. School schedule discussions and street market negotiations in non-English languages occur every day in our country as well as in the "far-off" lands portrayed in textbooks. And the future seems to promise an increasing frequency of such encounters, to the point of being part of a national routine. Ensuring that such common occurrences are not qualified as "foreign" is the responsibility of language educators teaching one of the essential, core subjects.

MACROCONTEXTUALIZATION

The future of world language education in the United States will depend in large part on the ability of language curricularists and researchers to begin to connect both curriculum and instruction to the individual societal setting within which education in language takes place. How classes are organized and conducted in St. Petersburg, Florida, or Carmel, California, or Throgs Neck, New York, will differ as a result of the differences in these settings in terms of factors like linguistic diversity, among others. Though advances in understanding second language acquisition will indubitably continue to have their place in language pedagogy, I argue that language courses will need to engage in the process of macrocontextualization. Macrocontextualization is the process of planning and implementing language instruction by incorporating the local political, economic, and cultural factors relating to linguistic diversity with the intent of developing students' skills in understanding the role that language plays in society. Beyond current goals of simply developing marginal skills in the language, students acquire an awareness of how language issues function in their society to both empower and discriminate against various segments of people. Macrocontextualization is related to two concepts discussed in the literature.

Henry Giroux and Peter McLaren (see McLaren 1998) have discussed the differences between micro-objectives and macro-objectives, with the latter related to connecting classroom objectives to external social realities. Shrum and Glisan (1994) and others have argued for contextualizing language instruction. In fact, contextualizing language instruction exhibits significant promise in terms of improving pedagogical practice, by allowing students to take advantage of the natural redundancy of language as they learn and acquire it.

As Omaggio (1986) pointed out in perhaps the most influential language methods text of our time,

Second language learners must be made aware of the conventions and constraints of discourse in the target language if they are to fully understand and communicate with the speakers of that language. The role of sociocultural factors, such as appropriate style or register of speech to be used in a given situation, needs to be taught overtly at various points along the course of the curriculum. . . . While our linguistic and pedagogical traditions have concentrated on the sentence for the purpose of analysis and instruction, it seems clear that language teaching in the years to come must concentrate on the wider contexts of authentic language use and actively teach discourse skills in the classroom. (117)

The concept of contextualization as currently expressed by language educators, however, is better termed microcontextualization, since it is within the confines of the language and the objectives of the classroom that the contextualization is taking place. Contextualized language instruction as currently practiced, however, tends to ignore the most significant contextual factor in language learning, the social setting in which it takes place. Omaggio's assertion about wider contexts is indeed correct, and one should add that not only discourse skills, but also an awareness of representations of subordinate and superordinate cultures in dominant discourse should be introduced to our students.

Macrocontextualization in the world language classroom engages the students and the teacher in the process of subjectifying the curriculum. In the words of the *Standards for Foreign Language Learning*, the goal of world language instruction is to help students know "how, when, and why to say what to whom" (National Standards in Foreign Language Education Project 1996, 11). Macrocontextualization adds to this tenet that first students should understand "whose how," "whose when," and "whose why." Ignoring these elements risks placing language educators at the heart of social reproductive activity diametrically opposed to their ideals of promoting tolerance of diversity along with language proficiency, as discussed in this text and evidenced by the concepts embodied in the *foreignness* agenda.

Macrocontextualization also serves to move language educators beyond the "grammar dilemma," by shifting focus from the internal mechanics of language use to external factors. The "grammar dilemma" refers to that tension faced by educators as they realize that instruction in language requires some understanding of the underlying structure. On the other hand, language teachers recognize that communicative goals often require de-emphasizing grammar. By macrocontextualizing language instruction, however, we argue that being able to use the language with any degree of fluency is of secondary concern, *for a time*.

World language instruction will first need to shirk the connections to greater liberal education tenets, not because they do not have some validity, but because these frameworks, when applied in contemporary educational institutions, support curricular and instructional practices that continue along the lines of *foreignness*. The well-educated language student of this society will need to understand as a primary goal the nature of language in societal relations. Thus, macrocontextualization will result in a renewed understanding of the importance of language skills, and then the educational structures (e.g., when language learning begins, how many years of study are appropriate) can be altered effectively to encourage the development of credible, communicative linguistic skills. In essence, once macrocontextualization increases the perceived relevance of language education to students and society, increasing proficiency in world languages will find broader social support.

Primary in the minds of language educators now should be a pedagogical shift toward the sociology of language. World language education will no longer strive to produce competent speakers of language as a solitary goal. The macrocontextualized courses will first move from an emphasis on the word, to the world (see Freire and Macedo 1987). As an integral component, macrocontextualization of world language education involves challenging existing disciplinary lines. The distinction between ESL, bilingual, and "foreign" language courses is, as discussed, more sociological than methodological. Though one could argue that the goals of the courses are decidedly different, this distinction is reflective of their differing sociological roles.

ESL and bilingual education, for example, typically are similar in that they seek to have students develop proficiency in English. Commonly contrasting Basic Interpersonal Communicative Skills (BICS) and Cognitive-Academic Language Proficiency (CALP) (see Cummins 1980, 1984), the practitioners differ with regard to the ways they treat the native language. Additive bilingualism tends to develop linguistic skills complementary to each other; whereas, subtractive bilingualism tends to develop target language proficiency at the expense of the other language(s), as is often the case in stand-alone ESL (see Carrasquillo and Rodriguez, 1996).

Foreign language classes, as Osborn and Reagan (1998) have argued, typically only intend to develop BICS, and that itself is an often unrealized goal. The assumed need to communicate is superficial at best, and as discussed within this text, results in benefits typically attributed to language study being supplanted by elements contributing to the *foreignness* framework. As I have stressed previously, combining these endeavors—ESL, bilingual education, foreign language education—into a single discipline referred to as world language education and including courses in American English for non-native speakers, the new discipline itself becomes more reflective of the diversity in languages found in the United States. This configuration allows for collaborative connections to be made between teachers and students of the languages as well.

Cooperative enterprises among English language learners and both native and non-native English speakers are not without precedent. Bromley (1995) suggests using a discourse diary, called a *buddy journal*, wherein an ESL student participates in a written conversation with a native English-speaking peer. Stern (1996) documents a peer tutoring program aimed at curbing the dropout rate and suggests that such a program could stem this problem in the Latino student population.

Nerenz and Knop (1982) suggest that a non-native student could be paired with a "buddy" native speaker, the latter acting as a tutor to the former. Of interest, in 1982 the Central States Conference on the Teaching of Foreign Languages focused on bridging the gap between ESL and foreign language teachers with its theme, Foreign Languages and English as a Second Language: From Monologue to Dialogue. Most of the proceedings focused on teachers from the two disciplines working together in the development and exchange of ideas (Garfinkel 1982).

In my own experience, I am aware of a foreign language teacher from Plainfield (Connecticut) High School who worked with an ESL teacher at Windham (Connecticut) High School in a program through Eastconn, the regional educational service agency. The students of each class exchanged e-mail and videos produced in English and Spanish. The students also became pen pals for each other and communicated via mail. Further, the students visited each other's schools for approximately half a day, talked, and celebrated a "fiesta" (R. T. Jones, personal communication, November 6, 1996).

The goal of the exchange was that students would "integrate their second language and culture," and it included the following objectives for students cited in a program overview:

Develop new culturally diverse relationships among the students from the two schools. Use and develop their second language skills in the context of community service. Develop a deeper awareness of the importance of having a second language to enhance communication. Develop interpersonal communications skills and group dynamic skills. Model the importance and enjoyment of cultural diversity. (Jones, personal communication, 1996)

Activities also included "reading and interpreting literature in their second language. Writing critiques of the reading using correct grammar and pronunciation." Students were reportedly very enthusiastic about the program. One teacher reports that one student took advanced Spanish in hopes that the teacher was going to "have another 'thing' with those other kids" and another reported that the greatest benefits of the exchange are increased cultural understanding and enhancement of second language skills (Jones, personal communication, 1996).

Experimental programs such as these highlight teachers who understand the need and applicability of language study in the United States. Curricular reforms at all levels need to be geared toward incorporating the realities of linguistic diversity in the language classrooms, the school, the community, the state, the region, and the nation. This approach of directing focus on expanding geographic circles allows for the discipline to develop uniform pedagogical and methodological approaches that are applied differently, based on the local linguistic context.

The challenge of developing national standards and recommended educational practices for the macrocontextualized classroom lies in the reality that communities nationwide have differing social configurations in terms of linguistic diversity. Beyond an awareness that language education must sometimes vary due to linguistic elements (e.g., at which level to introduce the subjunctive mood, based on frequency of use), the sociological setting in which these classes are conducted must also be taken into account. Therefore, curricular and instructional proposals from universities or state educational regulators must be seen as advisory. Critically reflective world language teachers can then apply their insights and the mandates in a way that reflects their best professional judgment. Their ability to do so, in turn, should be at the heart of U.S. curricular and instructional reform in language education in the coming century (see, for example, Popkewitz 1991).

Regardless, however, of the outcome of any curricular movement, critical reflection continues to play an important role in monitoring and further refining the growth of the profession. Only when teachers learn to challenge and redefine the mental frameworks related to differences in language and culture as expressed in our classrooms, can language education take its place among the core subjects. Language education could enter into a virtual dialectic, in fact, with the other core disciplines in terms of underlying power relationships existent in the facets of language use. Ultimately, though the ideologies that underlie language domination also include promoting the concept of *foreignness* to the dominant language group, macrocontextualization in the world language classroom addresses the lack of curricular subjectification by placing the study in the local and sociohistorical framework within which it operates and allows for future shifts in pedagogy to be geared toward sociohistorical realities, not positivistic pedagogical advances rooted in second language acquisition theory.

RESEARCH

It is not at all uncommon to hear teachers from all disciplines discuss the gap they perceive between research and practice as expressed in academe. Language teachers as well have found that advances in linguistics and language education are difficult to implement in the classroom, and they even feel that their needs are being ignored in terms of academic research. It is not surprising, then, when language teachers "express impatience, bordering on hostility, with researchers and their work" (Van Lier 1988, 26). This gulf, however, is one that cannot be bridged effectively only by the publication of "classroom tricks and helpful hints." It is the fundamental reexamination of language education in the United States for which I am arguing that will begin to bridge the chasm.

Goodlad (1994) and others have discussed a process referred to as simultaneous renewal. Incorporating the symbiosis between research and practice and again shifting the mental frameworks that have defined our field for the past half century or longer, research teams of teachers and professors can together begin to reinvigorate inquiry in language education. Though certainly critical perspectives should be sought in all levels of research, it is the necessary collaboration between practitioners and theorists that is of primary importance, lest any renewal fall victim to the charge of "ivory tower nonsense."

Perhaps the most effective way in which to implement these partnerships is through the development of research teams. Teachers and professors can work collaboratively in a number of research venues. Considering that teacher–classroom-based research is at times isolated, a professor could facilitate sequential or coordinated studies that address questions related to curricular and instructional reforms. If several teachers, independently, began to examine some of the same research questions related to praxis, the likelihood that the results could be applied in other settings may be increased. Obviously, I am arguing here for qualitative and critical research rather than empirical studies.

Language researchers will need to begin studying language in the community and the interrelationships between language in U.S. society and language education in the schools. We are not completely aware, for example, of how attitudes regarding linguistic diversity are reproduced or reflected within the educational context. Which attitudes, the educational or the broader sociocultural, tend to predominate? In which ways are they dissimilar or complementary? What roles do the teachers' and students' own preconceived attitudes play on the language learning environment? Certainly the teacher's messages, both explicit and implicit, to the students about the language and the people who speak it are of critical importance. How is language acquisition affected in terms of learning in differing social contexts? The reexamination of our praxis will need to seek answers to these and many other questions. Failing to effectively do so will not only result in the continued failure of language education in the United States, but will prevent the discipline from any real impact in a current movement to be included in the core curriculum of schools.

Researchers as well need to consider how the "failure" of the profession is related to issues of classroom management, the research-practice gap (perceived or real), and teacher security or insecurity with their own language proficiency. Classroom management issues may play a larger role in the maintenance of grammar syllabi than realized, since grammar lends itself well to worksheets and seatwork. Though grammar may not be most beneficial in terms of language learning, it does assist the teachers in their roles as behavior managers. This role is increasingly the one teachers are pressured to take.

And finally, in terms of critical educational research, developing a critical theory of language education that is broader-based than the insights presented in this text is needed as well. Insights in terms of language policy and planning, sociolinguistics, historical and international case studies, and language acquisition theory can assist teachers and researchers as well in developing their skills in critical reflection and a move toward a more democratic praxis. Such an endeavor would consider how what is known about language education, both in varying historical, economic, and political frames and from critical paradigmatic analysis, can be utilized in constructing a broader theoretical base from which further research and reform can proceed.

TEACHER EDUCATION

Teacher education of language teachers in the coming millennium should also embrace the issues raised by critical reflection on the state of the profession. Beyond simply incorporating ESL and bilingual instruction into the program, teacher education will need to focus on issues of applied sociolinguistics. Reagan (1997a) has argued that an awareness of these advances is prudent for all teachers; how much more so for those in language education. Additionally, Andrews' (1997) text *Language Exploration and Awareness*, Lippi-Green's (1997) *English with an Accent* and Ricento and Burnaby's (1998) *Language and Politics in the United States and Canada: Myths and Realities* can serve as appropriate introductions to the issues under discussion until one directed specifically at world language educators in the United States can be produced.

Teacher education will need to encourage teachers to view themselves as part of the research and renewal process for the profession. They will need to find support for exchange of classroom ideas, much as they do now in local, regional, and national conferences. The organizations hosting these meetings should renew their efforts at supporting teacher to teacher dialogue, incorporating the social issues in the classroom as well. One avenue in which teachers can shed new light on classroom practice and present it to others is through action research.

Marshall and Rossman (1995) point to four forms of research that share the characteristic of critiquing social relations, systems, and structures: democratic evaluation, neo-marxist ethnography, feminist research, and and participatory research. Using teacher-as-researcher

models and strategies, action researchers collaborate with the participants in posing applicable questions and gathering data.

Action researchers, among others, abandon the pretense of neutrality, choosing instead to focus on research results that are trustworthy
(LeCompte and Preissle 1993; Patton 1990). As Erlandson et al. (1993)
clarify,

> If intellectual inquiry is to have an impact on human knowledge,
> either by adding to an overall body of knowledge or by solving a
> particular problem, it must guarantee some measure of credibility
> about what it has inquired, must communicate in a manner that
> will enable application by its intended audience, and must enable
> its audience to check on its findings and the inquiry process by
> which the findings were obtained. . . . [W]e forget that our society
> has carefully decided, in some very important social arenas, to ob-
> tain, communicate, validate, and apply "truth" (or at least what is
> accepted for it) in alternative ways. (28)

Thus, if critical research about the classroom culture of the world language classroom is to be capable of bridging the gap between theorists
and practitioners within our discipline, the thrust of research must
originate in and be framed from within that classroom culture. Action
research has the capacity to engage the teachers themselves in the
search for trustworthy knowledge about the role of U.S. language education in broader cultural struggles.

I would further like to advocate a specific direction in participant research for world language education, which could be described as critical action research. Apple's (1995) call for marxist ethnographies and
Carspecken's (1996) text on critical ethnographic methods are appropriate for prolonged and university-level research. But teachers themselves, especially language teachers, will need research tools developed
for use at their levels and in their environments. Such could be the focus
of critical action research.

Carspecken (1996) has asserted the following regarding the power
of social groups within the social system:

> Clearly, some groups have greater amounts of [cultural] power
> than others, have much greater say in which forms of culture are to
> be taken seriously and employed widely and which forms are not.
> When examined carefully, one will see that cultural power inter-

sects in complex ways with . . . economic and political power. Groups enjoying extensive cultural power will also usually enjoy economic and political power. (191)

Given these realities, critical action research in language classrooms should focus on three core areas:

1. How cultural struggles, related to economic and political struggles, are reflected within language curricula and instructional practices, both explicitly and implicitly;
2. Ways that the nature and specifics of the cultural struggle can be illuminated for students; and
3. Methods by which praxis can challenge consent in the hegemonic relationships or meaning in ideological constructs that support these struggles.

Though simply illuminating the issues could be considered emancipatory knowledge, for teachers to move language education toward macrocontextualization will require the political activism of challenging theory and practice.

I have stressed the role of research in teacher education because I believe that in the renewal of the profession of language teacher, it is essential. Though one cannot deny the advances gained in understanding language acquisition and learning through research grounded in positivistic and interpretivistic frames of inquiry, one also cannot deny the need for critically reflective stances in the world language classroom. Just as naturalistic inquiry has been characterized as "fuzzy" or unorganized, some may claim the same of critical research and reflection in language education. I suggest that they would do well to remember the words of Charles Péguy: "*La tyrannie est toujours mieux organisée que la liberté.*"

CONCLUSION

Giroux (1997b) has noted that "the basis for a cultural politics and the struggle for power has been opened up to include the issues of language and identity" (204). Likewise, the traditions that typically frame research and practice in language education have competed with the realities of growing cultural interdependence and a shift in pressure to assimilate in some areas of public life in the United States. As a result, the

politics of cultural control have been either deemphasized or overlooked as most in the field have settled for technicist formulas or inquiry into the nature of language learning that springs from positivistic
or interpretivistic paradigms.

The argument that is being made in this text does not attempt to
flatly discredit that work. Instead, it is necessary that a new generation
of language educators expand that framework to consider the plethora
of variables that influence language learning. In the face of the expanding reality of pluralism within the United States, the task of language
educator is now to incorporate into classroom discourse the native
speakers in the United States, who exist in a definite political, historical,
and economic position. These native speakers are not merely resources,
they are representatives of and represented by cultural elements. In recognizing its place as a mediator of cultural capital, the language classroom becomes an agent for positive change within the struggle. The
field of language education has been one of enormous challenge in
most all sociocultural and historical contexts. Indeed, most recognize
that, even under optimum conditions, non-native language learning is
difficult. Every day, language teachers throughout the country enter
classrooms to attempt what seems to be impossible.

But in the shadow of such pessimistic odds, renewal of our professional vision in the twentieth century occurred with surprising regular-
ity. With such a rich history of effort behind us, the challenges of critical
reflection and language education may give one pause, but the greatest
traditions of the profession will drive us to rise to the challenge in the
twenty-first century. As I was reading one state's language curriculum
guide, I was struck by a claim the authors made that was bold, but perhaps prophetic: "[World language education] is unsurpassed in its
power to liberate the mind and spirit from the prisons of cultural pro-
vincialism, servile ideological conformity, and social class distinctions,
thereby freeing the individual person to think for herself or himself"
(Idaho State Department of Education 1994, 22). This sentiment,
though perhaps idealistic and lofty, can begin to be more credible every
day. And critical reflection in the language classroom will serve as a
powerful means to that end.

NOTE

1. I have chosen to employ the term *world language education* to describe
the learning of a language, including English, by a non-native speaker of the

language. World language should be differentiated from language of wider communication (LWC) or an international *lingua franca*, and a global language such as Esperanto. Though "second language" might also qualify as an appropriate marker, it seems to assume that all students enter the class as monolinguals.

Bibliography

Ackerman, D. 1989. Intellectual and practical criteria for successful curriculum integration. In *Interdisciplinary curriculum: Design and implementation*, ed. H. Jacobs, 25–38. Alexandria, VA: Association for Supervision and Curriculum Development.

Althusser, L. 1969. *For Marx*. New York: Vintage Books.

Andrews, L. 1997. *Language exploration and awareness*. Mahwah, NJ: Lawrence Erlbaum Associates.

Anyon, J. 1979. Ideology and United States history textbooks. *Harvard Educational Review* 49 (3): 361–386.

———. 1997. *Ghetto schooling: A political economy of urban educational reform*. New York: Teachers College Press.

Apple, M. W. 1979. *Ideology and curriculum*. Boston: Routledge and Kegan Paul.

———. 1988. *Teachers and texts*. New York: Routledge and Kegan Paul.

———. 1993. *Official knowledge: Democratic education in a conservative age*. New York: Routledge.

———. 1995. *Education and power*. 2d ed. New York: Routledge.

———. 1996. *Cultural politics and education*. New York: Teachers College Press.

Apple, M. W., and L. K. Christian-Smith, eds. 1991. *The politics of the textbook*. New York: Routledge.

Arnowitz, S., and H. Giroux. 1985. *Education under siege: The conservative, liberal, and radical debate over schooling.* South Hadley, MA: Bergin and Garvey.

————. 1991. *Postmodern education: Politics, culture, and social criticism.* Minneapolis: University of Minnesota Press.

Auerbach, E. R. 1995. The politics of the ESL classroom: Issues of power in pedagogical choices. In *Power and inequality in language education,* ed. J. W. Tollefson, 9–33. Cambridge, UK: Cambridge University Press.

Babb, V. S., S. L. Mendes, and K. E. Entzi. 1996. *¡Hablemos español!* Fargo, ND: Public Prairie Television.

Barzun, J. 1954. *Teacher in America.* Garden City, NY: Doubleday Anchor Books.

Bassey, M. O. 1996. Teachers as cultural brokers in the midst of diversity. *Educational Foundations* 10(2):37–52.

Bayreuth, L., and M. Manning. 1992. *Multicultural education of children and adolescents.* Needham Heights, MA: Allyn and Bacon.

Benesch, S. 1993. ESL, ideology, and the politics of pragmatism. *TESOL Quarterly* 27(4):705–717.

Bernstein, B. 1990. *The structuring of pedagogic discourse.* Volume IV, *Class, codes, and control.* New York: Routledge.

Beyer, L. E., and M. W. Apple, eds. 1988. *The curriculum: Problems, politics and possibilities.* Albany: State University of New York Press.

Biesta, G.J.J. 1998. Say you want a revolution . . . Suggestions for the impossible future of critical pedagogy. *Educational Theory* 48(4):499–510.

Böse, M., N. Lademann, and D. Schneider. 1989. *English for you: Englisches Lehrbuch, Teil V.* 4th ed. Berlin: Volk und Wissen Volkseigener Verlag.

Bromidge, W., and J. Burch. 1993. *Learning to communicate. In focus: The languages classroom. Teacher's notes.* London: Centre for Information on Language Teaching and Research.

Bromley, K. 1995. Buddy journals for ESL and native-English-speaking students. *TESOL Journal* 4(3):7–11.

Brookfield, S. D. 1995. *Becoming a critically reflective teacher.* San Francisco: Jossey-Bass.

Brosh, H. 1993. The influence of language status on language acquisition: Arabic in the Israeli setting. *Foreign Language Annals* 26 (3):347–358.

————. 1997. The sociocultural message of language textbooks: Arabic in the Israeli setting. *Foreign Language Annals* 30(3):311–326.

Brown, E. E. 1926. *The making of our middle school.* New York: Longman.

Brubacher J. W., C. W. Case, and T. G. Reagan. 1994. *Becoming a reflective educator: How to build a culture of inquiry in the schools.* Thousand Oaks, CA: Corwin Press.

Byram, M. 1989. *Cultural studies in foreign language education*. Clevedon, UK: Multilingual Matters.

Byram, M., and V. Esarte-Sarries. 1991. *Investigating cultural studies in foreign language teaching: A book for teachers*. Clevedon, UK: Multilingual Matters.

Byram, M., and C. Morgan. 1994. *Teaching-and-learning and language-and-culture*. Clevedon, UK: Multilingual Matters.

California Department of Education. 1989. *Foreign language framework*. Sacramento, CA: Author.

Carrasquillo, A. L., and V. Rodriguez. 1996. *Language minority students in the mainstream classroom*. Bristol, PA: Multilingual Matters.

Carspecken, P. F. 1996. *Critical ethnography in educational research: A theoretical and practical guide*. New York: Routledge.

Cazabon, M. J., N. A. Humbach, J. B. Fernández, and D. M. Koch, 1990. *Nosotros, los jóvenes*. Orlando, FL: Harcourt Brace Jovanovich.

Center for Applied Linguistics. 1995. *National profile of the United States. International Association for the Evaluation of Educational Achievement Language Education Study*. Washington, DC: Author.

Chick, J. K. 1996. Further thoughts on the adequacy of communicative competence as the goal of language teaching in a multilingual, multicultural society. *Journal for Language Teaching of the South African Association for Language Teaching* 30(4):322–332.

Coleman, H., ed. 1996. *Society and the language classroom*. Cambridge, UK: Cambridge University Press.

Connor, L. B. 1995. What Illinois teachers do in the classroom: New research. *I.C.T.F.L.—Accents* 8 (2):6–8.

Connors, B. 1984. A multicultural curriculum as action for social justice. In *Bilingual and multicultural education: Canadian perspectives*, ed. S. Shapson and V. D'Oyley, 104–111. Philadelphia: Multilingual Matters.

Cooper, R. L. and B. Spolsky, eds. 1991. *The influence of language on culture and thought: Essays in honor of Joshua A. Fishman's sixty-fifth birthday*. Berlin: Mouton de Gruyter.

Corson, D. 1989. Foreign language policy at school level: FLT and cultural studies across the curriculum. *Foreign Language Annals* 22 (4): 323–338.

———. 1990. *Language policy across the curriculum*. Clevedon, UK: Multilingual Matters.

Cranston Public Schools. 1989. *Foreign language curriculum 7–12*. Cranston, RI: Author.

Cummins, J. 1980. The construct of language proficiency in bilingual education. In *Georgetown University round table on languages and linguistics: Issues in bilingual education*, ed. J. Alatis, 81–103. Washington, DC: Georgetown University Press.

————. 1984. *Bilingualism and special education*. Clevedon, UK: Multilingual Matters.

Daniels, H. A. 1990. The roots of language protectionism. In *Not only English: Affirming America's multilingual heritage*, ed. H. A. Daniels, 3–12. Urbana, IL: National Council of Teachers of English.

Darder, A. 1991. *Culture and power in the classroom: A critical foundation for bicultural education*. Westport, CT: Bergin and Garvey.

Davis, V. I. 1990. Paranoia in language politics. In *Not only English: Affirming America's multilingual heritage*, ed. H. A. Daniels, 71–76. Urbana, IL: National Council of Teachers of English.

Department of Education and Science. 1990. *A survey of the teaching and learning of modern foreign languages in a sample of inner city and urban schools, spring term, 1989*. Middlesex, England: Department of Education and Science, Publications Dispatch Center.

Dicker, S. J. 1996. *Languages in America: A pluralist view*. Clevedon, UK: Multilingual Matters.

d'Usseau, E. R., and J. DeMado. 1996. *Allez, viens! Holt French level 1*. Annotated teacher's ed. Austin, TX: Holt, Rinehart and Winston.

Dyson, F. J. 1988. *Infinite in all directions: Gifford lectures given at Aberdeen, Scotland, April-November 1985*. New York: Harper and Row.

Eastman, C. M. 1983. *Language planning: An introduction*. San Francisco: Chandler and Sharp.

Ellis, R. 1990. *Understanding second language acquisition*. Oxford: Oxford University Press.

Erlandson, D. A., E. L. Harris, B. L. Skipper, and S. D. Allen. 1993. *Doing naturalistic inquiry: A guide to methods*. Newbury Park, CA: Sage.

Fairclough, N. 1989. *Language and power*. London: Longman.

Fishman, J. A. 1991. *Reversing language shift*. Clevedon, UK: Multilingual Matters.

Fitzgerald, J. 1993. Literacy and students who are learning English as a second language. *Reading Teacher* 38: 512–515.

Freire, P. 1985. *The politics of education: Culture, power, and liberation*. South Hadley, MA: Bergin and Garvey.

Freire, P., and D. Macedo. 1987. *Literacy: Reading the word and the world*. South Hadley, MA: Bergin and Garvey.

Galloway, V., D. Joba, and A. Labarca. 1998. *¡Acción! Level 1*. 2d ed. New York: Glencoe McGraw-Hill.

Garfinkel, A., ed. 1982. *ESL and the foreign language teacher: Report of central states conference on the teaching of foreign languages*. Skokie, IL: National Textbook Company.

Gates, H. L., Jr. 1992. *Loose canons: Notes on the culture wars*. New York: Oxford University Press.

Gee, J. 1996. *Social linguistics and literacies: Ideology in discourse*. 2d ed. London: Taylor and Francis.

Gersten, R. 1996. The double demands of teaching English language learners. *Educational Leadership* 53(5):18–22.

Geuss, R. 1981. *The idea of a critical theory: Habermas and the Frankfurt School*. Cambridge: Cambridge University Press.

Giroux, H. A. 1983. *Theory and resistance in education: A pedagogy for the opposition*. Boston: Bergin and Garvey.

———. 1988. *Teachers as intellectuals: Toward a critical pedagogy of learning*. New York: Bergin and Garvey.

———. 1993. *Living dangerously: Multiculturalism and the politics of difference*. New York: Peter Lang.

———. 1997a. Multiculturalism and the politics of nationalism in the global age. *Cultural Circles*, 1:7–27.

———. 1997b. *Pedagogy and the politics of hope: Theory, culture and schooling*. Boulder, CO: Westview Press.

———, ed. 1991. *Postmodernism, feminism, and cultural politics: Redrawing educational boundaries*. Albany: State University of New York Press.

Goldhagen, D. J. 1996. *Hitler's willing executioners: Ordinary Germans and the Holocaust*. New York: Random House.

Goodlad, J. I. 1994. *Educational renewal: Better teachers, better schools*. San Francisco: Jossey-Bass.

Goodman, N. 1992. *Introduction to sociology*. New York: HarperPerennial.

Gramsci, A. 1972. *Selections from the prison notebooks of Antonio Gramsci*. Edited and translated by Q. Hoare and G. Nowell-Smith. New York: International Publishers.

Gutiérrez, J. R., H. L. Rosser, and M. Rosso-O'Laughlin. 1997. *¡Ya verás! Primer nivel*. 2d ed. Boston: Heinle and Heinle.

Habermas, J. 1972. *Knowledge and human interests*. 2d ed. Translated by J. J. Shapiro. London: Heinemann.

Hamayan, E. 1990. Preparing mainstream classroom teachers to teach potentially English proficient students. In *Proceedings of the first research symposium on limited English proficient students' issues*, 1–21. Washington, DC: Office of Bilingual Education and Minority Language Affairs.

Hamm, C. M. 1989. *Philosophical issues in education: An introduction*. New York: Falmer Press.

Hendrie, C. 1997. N.Y. regents to drop foreign-language requirement. *Education Week* 17(5):3.

Hines, L. M. 1981. *Our Latin heritage*. 3d ed. Orlando, FL: Harcourt Brace Jovanovich.

Horwitz, E. 1996. Meeting the cognitive and emotional needs of foreign language teachers. In *Foreign language teacher education: Multiple perspectives*, ed. Z. Moore. Lanham, MD: University Press of America.

Idaho State Department of Education. 1994. *Idaho foreign languages content guide and framework.* Boise, ID: Author.

Irwin, J. W. 1996. *Empowering ourselves and transforming schools: Educators making a difference.* Albany: State University of New York Press.

Jacobs, H. H., ed. 1989. *Interdisciplinary curriculum: Design and implementation.* Alexandria, VA: Association for Supervision and Curriculum Development.

Jameson, F. 1971. *Marxism and form.* Princeton, NJ: Princeton University Press.

Jarvis, G. A., D. W. Birckbichler, T. M. Bonin, and L. C. Shih. 1989. *¿Y Tú?* Austin, TX: Holt, Rinehart and Winston.

Johnson, R. 1991. A new road to serfdom: A critical history of the 1988 act. In *Education Limited,* ed. Education Group II, 31–86. London: Unwin Hyman.

Kanpol, B. 1999. *Critical Pedagogy: An Introduction.* 2d ed. Westport, CT: Bergin & Garvey.

Kelman, H. C. 1971. Language as an aid and barrier to involvement in the national system. In *Can language be planned? Sociolinguistic theory and practice for developing nations,* ed. J. Rubin and B. H. Jernudd, 21–51. Honolulu: University of Hawaii Press.

Kozol, J. 1991. *Savage inequalities: Children in America's schools.* New York: HarperPerennial.

Kramsch, C. 1993. *Context and culture in language teaching.* Oxford: Oxford University Press.

Kress, G., and R. Hodge. 1979. *Language as ideology.* London: Routledge and Kegan Paul.

Kumaravadivelu, B. 1994. The postmodern condition: (E)merging strategies for second/foreign language teaching. *TESOL Quarterly* 28 (1): 27–48.

Lafayette, R., ed. 1996. *National standards: A catalyst for reform.* Lincolnwood, IL: National Textbook Company.

Lambert, W. E. 1974. An alternative to the foreign language teaching profession. In *Essays on the teaching of culture,* ed. H. B. Altman and V. E. Hanzeli, 55–77. Detroit, MI: Advancement Press of America.

Lanigan, R. L. 1981. A critical theory approach. In *Handbook of political communication,* ed. D. D. Nimmo and K. R. Sanders, 141–168. Beverly Hills, CA: Sage.

Lawton, D. 1975. *Class, culture and the curriculum.* London: Routledge and Kegan Paul.

LeCompte, M. D. and J. Preissle. 1993. *Ethnography and qualitative design in educational research.* 2d ed. San Diego, CA: Academic Press.

Lessow-Hurley, J. 1996. *The foundations of dual language instruction.* 2d ed. White Plains, NY: Longman.

Lippi-Green, R. 1997. *English with an accent: Language, ideology, and discrimination in the United States.* London: Routledge.

Little, J. W. 1993. Teachers' professional development in a climate of educational reform. *Educational Evaluation and Policy Analysis* 15 (2):129–151.

Littlewood, W. 1981. *Communicative language teaching.* Cambridge, UK: Cambridge University Press.

Lonning, R. A., T. C. DeFranco, and T. P. Weinland. 1998. Development of theme-based, interdisciplinary, integrated curriculum: A theoretical model. *School Science and Mathematics* 98(6):312–318.

Lucy, J. A. 1996. The scope of linguistic relativity: An analysis and review of empirical research. In *Rethinking linguistic relativity*, ed. J. J. Gumperz and S. C. Levinson, 37–69. Cambridge, UK: Cambridge University Press.

Macedo, D. 1994. *Literacies of power: What Americans are not allowed to know.* Boulder, CO: Westview Press.

Marshall, C., and G. B. Rossman. 1995. *Designing qualitative research.* 2d ed. Thousand Oaks, CA: Sage.

Marx, K. 1972. *The German ideology.* New York: International Publishers.

Mason, K., and K. Nicely. 1995. Pronouns of address in Spanish-language textbooks: The case for *vos*. *Foreign Language Annals* 28 (3):360–370.

Maxim, H. H. 1998. Authorizing the foreign language student. *Foreign Language Annals* 31(3):407–420.

Mayer, J. 1993. How the system is used to make meaning. In *Linguistics for teachers*, ed. L. Cleary and M. Linn. New York: McGraw-Hill, Inc.

McDonough, S. 1981. *Psychology in foreign language teaching.* London: Allen and Unwin.

McLaren, P. 1989. *Life in schools: An introduction to critical pedagogy in the foundations of education.* New York: Longman.

———. 1997. *Revolutionary multiculturalism.* Boulder, CO: Westview Press.

———. 1998. *Life in schools: An introduction to critical pedagogy in the foundations of education.* 3d ed. New York: Longman.

McRobbie, A. 1978. Working class girls and the culture of femininity. In *Women take issue*, ed. Women's Studies Group, 96–108. London: Hutchinson.

Met, M., R. S. Sayers, and C. E. Wargin. 1996. *Paso a paso 1.* Teacher's ed. Glenview, IL: Scott, Foresman.

Milk, R., C. Mercado, C. and A. Sapiens. 1992. *Re-thinking the education of teachers of language-minority children: Developing reflective teachers for changing schools.* Washington, DC: National Clearinghouse for Bilingual Education.

Milroy, J., and L. Milroy. 1985. *Authority in language: Investigating language prescription and standardisation.* London: Routledge and Kegan Paul.

Monroe, P. 1940. *Founding of the American public school system.* New York: Macmillan.

Moore, Z. 1996. Culture: How do teachers teach it? In *Foreign language teacher education: Multiple perspectives,* ed. Z. Moore. Lanham, MD: University Press of America.

National Standards in Foreign Language Education Project. 1996. *Standards for foreign language learning: Preparing for the 21st century.* Lawrence, KS: Allen Press.

Nebraska Department of Education. 1996. *Nebraska K-12 foreign language frameworks.* Lincoln, NE: Author.

Nerenz, A. G., and C. K. Knop. 1982. The effect of group size on students' opportunity to learn in the second-language classroom. In *ESL and the foreign language teacher: Report of central states conference on the teaching of foreign languages,* ed. A. Garfinkel, 47–60. Skokie, IL: National Textbook Company.

New Jersey State Department of Education. 1992. *Core course proficiencies: Foreign languages.* Trenton, NJ: Author.

Newark Board of Education. 1994. *Secondary 1994: Italian 1 & 2.* Newark, NJ: Author.

North Dakota Department of Public Instruction. 1989. *Foreign language curriculum guide.* Bismarck, ND: Author.

Ohio Department of Education. 1996. *Foreign languages: Ohio's model competency-based program.* Columbus, OH: Author.

Omaggio, A. C. 1986. *Teaching language in context: Proficiency-oriented instruction.* Boston: Heinle and Heinle.

Ornstein, A. C. and F. P. Hunkins. 1993. *Curriculum foundations, principles and issues.* 2d ed. Boston: Allyn and Bacon.

Osborn, T. A. 1997. Power interactions and cultural reproduction in United States foreign language education. Paper read at the annual conference of the American Educational Studies Association, November 2, San Antonio, Texas.

———. 1998. Providing access: Foreign language learners and genre theory. *Foreign Language Annals* 31(1):40–47.

Osborn, T. A. and T. Reagan. 1998. Why Johnny can't *hablar, parler* or *sprechen:* Foreign language education and multicultural education. *Multicultural Education* 6 (2): 2–9.

Osborne, R. E. and S. Tilles. 1975. *Voces y vistas.* 2d ed. New York: Harper and Row.

Overfield, D. M. 1997. From the margins to the mainstream: Foreign language education and community-based learning. *Foreign Language Annals* 30(4):485–491.

Patton, M. 1990. *Qualitative evaluation and research methods.* 2d ed. Newbury Park, CA: Sage.

Peirce, B. N. 1995. Social identity, investment, and language learning. *TESOL Quarterly* 29:9–31.

Pennycook, A. 1995. English in the world/The world in English. In *Power and inequality in language education,* ed. J. W. Tollefson, 34–58. Cambridge, UK: Cambridge University Press.

Peters, R. S. 1975. Education and the educated man. In *A critique of current educational aims. Part I of Education and the development of reason,* ed. R. F. Dearden, P. H. Hirst, and R. F. Peters, 1–16. London: Routledge and Kegan Paul.

Phoenix Union High School District. 1993. *Curriculum guidelines: Spanish.* Phoenix, AZ: Phoenix Union High School District No. 210.

Pool, J. 1979. Language planning and identity planning. *International Journal of the Sociology of Language* 20:5–21.

Popkewitz, T. S. 1991. *A political sociology of educational reform: Power/knowledge in teaching, teacher education, and research.* New York: Teachers College Press.

Raphan, D., and M. Gertner. 1990. ESL and foreign language: A teaching and learning perspective. *Research and Teaching in Developmental Education* 6 (2):75–84.

Reagan, T. 1986. The role of language policy in South African education. *Language Problems and Language Planning* 10(1):1–13.

———. 1997a. The case for applied linguistics in teacher education. *Journal of Teacher Education* 48:185–196.

———. 1997b. When is a language not a language? Challenges to "linguistic legitimacy" in educational discourse. *Educational Foundations* 11(3):5–28.

Reagan, T. and K. Case, 1996. Linguistic pluralism for internationalization: The case for nontraditional approaches to language study for U.S. schools. In *Language status in the post-Cold War era,* ed. K. Müller, 97–107. Lanham, MD: University Press of America and the Center for Research and Documentation on World Language Problems.

Reagan, T. and T. A. Osborn. 1998. Power, authority, and domination in foreign language education: Toward an analysis of educational failure. *Educational Foundations* 12(2):45–62.

Ricento, T. 1988. The framers knew best. *TESOL Newsletter* 22(2).

———. 1998. National language policy in the United States. In *Language and politics in the United States and Canada: Myths and realities,* ed. T. Ricento and B. Burnaby, 85–112. Mahwah, NJ: Lawrence Erlbaum Associates.

Ricento, T. and B. Burnaby, eds. 1998. *Language and politics in the United States and Canada: Myths and realities.* Mahwah, NJ: Lawrence Erlbaum Associates.

Richards, J. C., and T. S. Rodgers. 1986. *Approaches and methods in language teaching: A description and analysis*. Cambridge, UK: Cambridge University Press.

Rigg, P., and V. Allen, eds. 1989. *When they don't all speak English: Integrating the ESL student into the regular classroom*. Urbana, IL: National Council of Teachers of English.

Rivers, W. 1988. *Communicating naturally in a second language*. New York: Cambridge University Press.

Rothstein, S. W. 1991. *Identity and ideology: Sociocultural theories of schooling*. New York: Greenwood Press.

Rousmaniere, K. 1997. *City teachers: Teaching and school reform in historical perspective*. New York: Teachers College Press.

Rubin, L. B. 1976. *Worlds of pain: Life in the working-class family*. New York: Basic Books.

Ruiz, H. 1987. The impregnability of textbooks: The example of American foreign language education. In *Initiatives in communicative language teaching II*, ed. S. Savignon and M. Berns, 33–53. Reading, MA: Addison-Wesley.

Said, E. W. 1978. *Orientalism*. New York: Vintage.

Samaniego, F. A., F. X. Alarcón, and R. Otheguy. 1997. *Tu Mundo: Primer curso para hispanohablantes*. Lexington, MA: D. C. Heath.

Scholl, I. 1983. *The White Rose: Munich 1942–43*. Translated by A. R. Schultz. Middletown, CT: Wesleyan University Press.

Schubert, W. H. 1996. Perspectives on four curriculum traditions. *Educational Horizons* 74: 169–176.

Scott, R. A. 1972. A proposed framework for analyzing deviance as a property of social order. In *Theoretical perspectives on deviance*, eds. R. A. Scott and J. D. Douglas, 9–36. New York: Basic Books.

Seelye, H. N. 1974. *Teaching culture*. Skokie, IL: National Textbook Company.

Shanahan, D. 1998. Culture, culture and "culture" in foreign language teaching. *Foreign Language Annals* 31(3):451–458.

Shor, I. 1986. *Culture wars: School and society in the conservative restoration 1969–1984*. Boston: Routledge and Kegan Paul.

Shrum, J. L. and E. W. Glisan. 1994. *Teacher's handbook: Contextualized language instruction*. Boston: Heinle and Heinle.

Simon, P. 1980. *The tongue-tied American: Confronting the foreign language crisis*. New York: Continuum.

Simone, M. 1993. The big change in teaching foreign languages. *Planning for Higher Education* 21 (3): 15–20.

Skutnabb-Kangas, T. 1981. *Bilingualism or not: The education of minorities*. Clevedon, UK: Multilingual Matters.

Smyth, W. J. 1992. Teachers' work and the politics of reflection. *American Educational Research Journal* 29(2):267–300.

Soder, R., ed. 1996. *Democracy, education, and the schools.* San Francisco: Jossey-Bass.

Solomon, J. 1997. Language teachers align curricula with standards: Preliminary results of a national survey. *ERIC/CLL News Bulletin* 21(1):1, 6–7.

South Carolina State Board of Education. 1993. *South Carolina foreign language framework.* Columbia, SC: Author.

State of Florida, Department of State. 1996. *Florida curriculum frameworks. Foreign languages: Pre-K-12 sunshine state standards and instructional practices.* Tallahassee, FL: Author.

Steinbach, P. 1990. *Gedenkstätte deutcher Widerstand/the German Resistance Memorial Center: Exhibition resistance to national socialism.* Translated by J. M. Grossman. Berlin: Helmich KG.

Stern, G. 1996. What to do about the Hispanic high school drop-out rate: Hispanic drop-out project takes the lead. *Hispanic Outlook* (September 13):5–6.

Stone, R. 1990. The motivation to study literature. *Babel* 25(3):18–21.

Strength through wisdom: A critique of U.S. capability. A report to the president from the president's commission on foreign language and international studies. 1979. Washington, DC: Government Printing Office.

Strike, K. A. and J. F. Soltis. 1992. *The ethics of teaching.* 2d ed. New York: Teachers College Press.

Swan, M. 1985a. A critical look at the communicative approach (1). *ELT Journal* 39(1):2–12.

——————. 1985b. A critical look at the communicative approach (2). *ELT Journal* 39(2):76–87.

Tannen, D. 1994. *Gender and discourse.* New York: Oxford University Press.

Tollefson, J. W. 1991. *Planning language, planning inequality: Language policy in the community.* London: Longman.

————, ed. 1995. *Power and inequality in language education.* New York: Cambridge University Press.

Tyack, D. B. 1974. *The one best system: A history of American urban education.* Cambridge, MA: Harvard University Press.

Valdman, A., G. MacMillin, M. LaVergne, and E. Gahala. 1986. *Son et Sens. Première Partie.* 3d ed. Teacher's annotated ed. Glenview, IL: Scott, Foresman.

Valette, J-P., and R. M. Valette. 1984. *Spanish for mastery I.* Lexington, MA: D. C. Heath.

Van Lier, L. 1988. *The classroom and the language learner: Ethnography and second-language classroom research,* 26. London: Longman. Quoting Seliger, H. W. and Long, M. H., eds. 1983. *Classroom oriented research in second language acquisition,* v. Rowley, MA: Newbury House.

Van Meter, J. 1990. Academic credit for ESL classes? *Review of Research in Developmental Education* 8(1):1–4.

Villa, D. J. 1996. Choosing a "standard" variety of Spanish for the instruction of native Spanish speakers in the U.S. *Foreign Language Annals* 29(2):191–200.

Wald, H. 1991. *Spanish is fun. Book 1. Lively lessons for beginners.* 2d ed. New York: Amsco School Publications.

Wicklund, R. A. and J. W. Brehm. 1976. *Perspectives on cognitive dissonance.* Hillsdale, NJ: Lawrence Erlbaum Associates.

Widdowson, H. G. 1985. Against dogma: A reply to Michael Swan. *ELT Journal* 39(3):158–161.

————. 1994. The ownership of English. *TESOL Quarterly* 28(2):377–389.

Wieczorek, J. A. 1994. The concept of "French" in foreign language texts. *Foreign Language Annals* 27(4):487–497.

Wiley, T. J. 1998. The imposition of World War I era English-only policies and the fate of German in North America. In *Language and politics in the United States and Canada: Myths and realities,* ed. T. Ricento and B. Burnaby, 211–242. Mahwah, NJ: Lawrence Erlbaum Associates.

Williams, R. 1977. *Marxism and literature.* New York: Oxford University Press.

Willis, P. 1977. *Learning to labour.* Lexington, MA: D. C. Heath.

Wink, J. 1997. *Critical pedagogy: Notes from the real world.* New York: Longman.

Winkler, G. 1995. *Komm mit! Holt German Level 1.* Teacher's ed. Austin, TX: Holt, Rinehart and Winston.

Wong, S. C. 1993. Promises, pitfalls, and principles of text selection in curricular diversification: The Asian-American case. In *Freedom's plow,* ed. T. Perry and J. Fraser, 109–120. New York: Routledge.

Wong-Fillmore, L. 1991a. Language and cultural issues in the early education of language minority children. In *The care and education of America's young children: Obstacles and opportunities. Ninetieth yearbook of the National Society for the Study of Education, Part II,* ed. S. Kagan, 30–49. Chicago: University of Chicago Press.

————. 1991b. Second language learning in children: A model of language learning in social context. In *Language processing in bilingual children,* ed. E. Balystok, 49–69. Cambridge, MA: Cambridge University Press.

Woodford, P. E., C. J. Schmitt, and R. H. Marshall. 1989. *McGraw-Hill Spanish amistades.* Annotated teacher's ed. New York: McGraw-Hill.

Wright, I., and C. LaBar. 1984. Multiculturalism and morality. In *Bilingual and multicultural education: Canadian perspectives,* ed. S. Shapson and V. D'Oyley, 112–129. Philadelphia: Multilingual Matters.

Zeichner, K. M. 1994. Research on teacher thinking and different views of reflective practice in teaching and teacher education. In *Teachers' minds and actions: Research on teachers' thinking and practice*. Bristol, PA: Falmer Press.

Index

About the Author

TERRY A. OSBORN is Assistant Professor, Secondary Education and Youth Services, Queens College, CUNY.

Printed in the United States
213159BV00003B/1/A

9 781593 113131